Care Staff
Management

JOHN CLEMENTS
and
EWA ZARKOWSKA

Care Staff
Management

A practitioner's guide

JOHN WILEY & SONS
Chichester · New York · Brisbane · Toronto · Singapore

Other Wiley Editorial Offices

John Wiley & Sons, Inc., 605 Third Avenue,
New York, NY 10158-0012, USA

Jacaranda Wiley Ltd, 33 Park Road, Milton,
Queensland 4064, Australia

John Wiley & Sons (Canada) Ltd, 22 Worcester Road,
Rexdale, Ontario M9W 1L1, Canada

John Wiley & Sons (SEA) Pte Ltd, 37 Jalan Pemimpin #05-04,
Block B, Union Industrial Building, Singapore 2057

Library of Congress Cataloging-in-Publication Data

Clements, John, 1946–
    Quality care : a guide to managing staff in the health care
professions / John Clements and Ewa Zarkowska.
        p.   cm.
    Includes bibliographical references and index.
    ISBN 0-471-94395-9 (paper)
    1. Health facilities—Personnel management—Handbooks, manuals,
etc.   2. Medical personnel—Mental health services—Handbooks,
manuals, etc.   I. Zarkowska, Ewa.   II. Title
    [DNLM: 1. Mental Health Services—organization & administration.
2. Community Health Services—organization & administration.
3. Personnel Management—methods.   WA 546.1   C626q   1994]
RA971.35.C55   1994
362.1'068'3—dc20
DNLM/DLC
for Library of Congress   93–39531
                                                                   CIP

British Library Cataloguing in Publication Data

A catalogue record for this book is available from the British Library

ISBN   0-471-94395-9

Typeset in 10/12pt Photina by Dorwyn Ltd, Rowlands Castle, Hants
Printed and bound in Great Britain by Redwood Books, Trowbridge, Wiltshire

CONTENTS

TO THE READER

This book is written to be dipped into on an 'as need' basis rather than be read from cover to cover. It is not meant as an academic text—dealing with theories of work, human motivation and behaviour. It is meant as an aid to problem solving and a source of practical ideas for hard pressed managers in those human services that seek to support and help people with long term disabilities—people with physical and/or learning disabilities, people with mental health problems, people experiencing the difficulties associated with old age.

Thus each chapter is relatively self contained and can be understood without reference to other chapters. The only possible exception to this relates to Chapter 2. This sets out the framework—the STAR model—that we use to organise and analyse the many influences on performance and satisfaction at work. It introduces, defines and illustrates the terms of the model—Setting conditions, Triggers, Actions, Results—terms that are used throughout the text. Thus a better understanding of each chapter may be gained if Chapter 2 has been read first. However, it is our hope that even if the reader omits Chapter 2 the other chapters will be comprehensible and a source of ideas for practical action.

A few other points need to be made about terminology and style.

➤ No attempt has been made to use he or she consistently.
➤ No attempt has been made to identify those who use the services that this book is concerned with by a consistent term—individuals, service users, clients, residents, people—are treated as equivalents and are used in no systematic way.
➤ The style of the book is deliberately 'cut up' so that extended passages of grammatical text are reduced. This is an attempt to make the book easier to dip in and out of and to make key points easier to remember. That is the intention—the reader will judge if the approach is successful.

ACKNOWLEDGEMENTS

This book would not have been complete without the involvement, encouragement and support of many people:

- the large number of service providers that we have worked with over the years
- our families and close friends (including the quadrupedal variety)
- the editorial team at Wiley

Our thanks go to all of these and we hope that the quality of the outcome is proportionate to the quality of the input that they have all provided.

John Clements
Ewa Zarkowska

SECTION I   **Introduction**

This section (Chapters 1 and 2) looks at some of the key features of services that seek to meet the needs of people with long term disabilities. It also introduces the STAR model, a problem solving framework for analysing human behaviour—in this case the functioning of people at work. It illustrates the range of variables that can influence performance and satisfaction; and that therefore constitute some of the levers which a manager can use to effect change with her staff.

CHAPTER 1　Key features of work in caring services

AIMS OF THE CHAPTER

1. To illustrate the kinds of services to whose needs this book is addressed.

2. To identify key characteristics of these services and the implications of these characteristics for the goals of management.

INTRODUCTION

This book looks at some of the tools available to managers in professional care services that will help them to get the best out of their staff. It is these staff that are paid to provide what is called 'care'. The recipients of such services are those who need unusual degrees of support in order to manage their everyday lives and in particular this book is concerned with those who have long term needs for such support.

There may be many reasons why one person needs extensive and extended support from others. These include

➤ Immaturity
➤ Pervasive learning difficulties (mental handicap)
➤ Severe motor impairments
➤ deteriorating physical/mental conditions (such as Alzheimer's disease)
➤ Chronic mental illness

Most such needs for support in Western industrialised countries are met within the family system. The involvement of paid staff can arise because of

➤ Legal requirements (such as that to provide education to children)
➤ Lack of availability of family resources
➤ A need for expertise/opportunities not available in the family system and thought to enhance the individual's quality of life (such as treatment services of various kinds)

In most Western societies there are very large numbers of people in receipt of paid care and likewise very large numbers of people paid to provide such services.

If this book is to consider how to promote quality in care services then some definition is needed of 'caring' for another. The coverage of this topic will not be comprehensive but will draw attention to features that are central to the perspective of this text.

ASPECTS OF CARE

Sustained Relationships

At the centre of one human being supporting another is the relationship between the two. Care is not reducible to mechanical activities that could be completed by machine, helpful though technology can be.

A walking frame does not remove the need for a physiotherapist.

A computer does not remove the need for a teacher.

An answering machine does not remove the need for someone to talk to.

The help experienced is determined to a very significant degree by the quality of the relationship between those involved. Trust and understanding are essential to helping/ supportive relationships. Given the long term nature of the needs with which this book is concerned, the relationships formed need to be seen as extended in time.

> **Good quality, sustained relationships between those who provide and those who use services are central to the care endeavour.**

Technical Skills

All those who offer support to another must be able to form and sustain relationships. However, depending upon the exact nature of the service and the needs that it is trying to address there will be a range of specific technical skills that are essential for providers. These might include knowing how to

➤ Assist the acceptance of food in a very physically handicapped person
➤ Communicate with someone who is deaf and blind
➤ Assist someone with learning difficulties to make choices about his or her life
➤ Counsel someone in a disturbed state
➤ Use systematic behaviour change techniques to help someone learn new ways of coping
➤ Hold and position someone to reduce involuntary movements
➤ Orient in space and time someone who is confused

> **Over and above general relationship skills, those paid to offer support will need technical skills so that they can achieve the more specific goals of entering the life of another.**

Complexity

The needs of those who use care services are often very difficult to identify. They will emerge from the interaction of at least four domains:

➤ Personal characteristics of the individual concerned
➤ The exact nature of the disabling condition that he or she experiences

➤   The reaction of the world to the individual
➤   The reaction of the individual to all of the above

Our understanding of these processes is limited albeit developing continually. Psychology is at an early stage of its development. The understanding of conditions such as cerebral palsy, autism, Alzheimer's disease, schizophrenia, general intellectual impairment and many other handicapping conditions is likewise evolving. However, it is clear that the progress to be made is very largely determined by the quality of work carried out on a day to day basis by those who have the primary face to face relationships with the individual affected. This point cannot be overemphasised.

The implications are that those providing services must be able to

➤   Tolerate uncertainty
➤   Take on readily and try out new ideas
➤   Accept variable progress and look for and celebrate small rather than spectacular changes
➤   Tolerate and work with the emotional distress often experienced by those affected
➤   Recognise and work with the emotional distress involved in caring for a damaged other

The nature of care work is complex and brings with it considerable stresses.

Teamwork

Paid carers, unlike family carers, work limited hours. Trying to meet the needs of an individual

24 hours a day
seven days a week
52 weeks a year

or any considerable proportion thereof, requires complex organisations involving many individuals. If the user is to experience maximum quality and benefit from the service it is essential that those individuals act in a coordinated, comprehensible way.

Those who provide services have to be able to work with others and develop a team rather than an individual approach to meeting the needs of users.

CONCLUSIONS

For Staff

Those who work as carers must be able to

➤   Form and sustain individual relationships with users
➤   Acquire and use whatever technical skills are needed

➤ Take on new knowledge and skills
➤ Manage constructively personal emotional distress
➤ Work together with others to deliver a coherent service

For Managers

Alongside all the other tasks that fall under the heading of management, the manager of a care service must be able to get staff to

➤ Come to work regularly
➤ Act skilfully with users
➤ Take on new knowledge and skills
➤ Acknowledge and manage constructively personal emotional distress
➤ Work well with other staff

and keep on doing all the above.

These psychological aspects of management are the focus of this book. The starting point will be to suggest a framework that will help to organise these efforts in a coherent way.

SUMMARY

1. THIS BOOK IS CONCERNED WITH THOSE WHO HAVE LONG TERM NEEDS FOR EXTENSIVE SUPPORT FROM OTHERS.

2. SUCH SUPPORT WORK REQUIRES GOOD QUALITY, SUSTAINED RELATIONSHIPS BETWEEN THOSE WHO USE AND THOSE WHO PROVIDE SERVICES.

3. RELATIONSHIP ORIENTED WORK NEEDS TO BE COMBINED WITH THE USE OF RELEVANT TECHNICAL SKILLS.

4. THE NATURE OF SUCH WORK IS COMPLEX AND STRESSFUL.

5. QUALITY SERVICES REQUIRE STAFF TO WORK TOGETHER AND TO DEVELOP A TEAM APPROACH TO MEETING INDIVIDUAL NEEDS.

6. ENABLING STAFF TO FUNCTION IN THE WAYS OUTLINED IN 2–5 ARE THE MANAGEMENT TASKS THAT THIS BOOK ADDRESSES.

CHAPTER 2   **Understanding people at work—the STAR model**

AIMS OF THE CHAPTER

1. To ILLUSTRATE IMPORTANT CONSTITUENTS OF QUALITY IN HUMAN SERVICE WORK.

2. To DESCRIBE THE INFLUENCES OVER INDIVIDUAL FUNCTIONING AT WORK.

3. To PRESENT THE STAR FRAMEWORK FOR ANALYSING THE FACTORS WHICH INFLUENCE FUNCTIONING AT WORK.

INTRODUCTION

The quality of any product or service is dependent to varying degrees upon the functioning of the staff directly involved in the production or delivery process. However, in the human service field the dependence is near complete. As discussed in Chapter 1,

human services are about relationships

This means that their quality is

to a very large extent determined by those who form the relationships

the staff who work day to day with those who use the service. Thus the functioning of staff, both individually and as a working group, is the central issue in delivering quality services.

KEY ASPECTS OF WORK FUNCTIONING

There are two aspects of staff functioning which it is important to consider.

1. Job satisfaction. The extent to which a staff member enjoys work and feels positively about it. This is particularly related to how long an individual will stick at a job.

2. Job performance. How well the staff member actually does the job, how effective he is. These are rather different concepts.

Example

Service: A day service specialising in helping adults with learning difficulties who experience additional behavioural and emotional problems.

Vignette 1

The service is run in a very democratic and supportive way. The key emphasis is upon support and allowing choice to both providers and users. The work space is open plan allowing a lot of contact throughout the day. There are weekly unstructured discussions on all users and a weekly staff support group. There are no formal programmes of work with users. There are frequent training days for staff with a lot of time devoted to team building. All staff have personal supervision sessions. The manager is frequently present in the workplace, encouraging and supporting staff.

Likely functioning of staff: high statisfaction
low performance

Vignette 2

The service is run in terms of achieving specific goals with users. Decision making is participative but the manager will have the final say in case of disagreements. There are weekly structured discussions on each user and each user has a set of clear goals to which formal programmes of work are directed. There are occasional training days but a lot of use is made of open learning approaches so that much staff development goes on outside of work hours. All staff have personal supervision sessions. The manager is frequently present in the workplace, encouraging and supporting staff but is also quick to pick up on any practices deemed inappropriate.

Likely functioning of
staff: moderate satisfaction
high performance

Vignette 3

The service has no clear purpose and no clear systems of work. Staff are left to do whatever they think is appropriate and there are marked differences of opinion between staff on this. There are no regular meetings other than the annual reviews. There are occasional training days although these do not usually have much to do with the needs of the clients who use the service. The manager is not often present in the workplace and seems primarily concerned with budgetary issues.

Likely functioning of staff: low satisfaction
low performance

Human service work is

➤ Based upon sustained relationships
➤ Developmental in orientation, seeking to enhance quality of life and maximise levels of personal functioning

It is thus a complex enterprise requiring high levels of

- ➤ Continuity
- ➤ Staff skill

Understanding the determinants of both satisfaction and performance are essential if a service is to have staff who function well—and keep on doing so.

As the vignettes illustrate, satisfaction and performance very much depend upon characteristics of the workplace. Those characteristics that can be influenced by managers constitute the focus of this book.

THE INFLUENCES ON PERFORMANCE AND SATISFACTION

Traditional Views

There are many theories about

- ➤ Why people work
- ➤ What determines how well they work

It has been said that people work *either* to get money *or* to fulfil themselves. One popular view is that the motivations that influence people can be organised into a neat hierarchy—as the more basic needs related to physical survival (such as food and shelter) are met, more sophisticated needs (such as personal development) become important. Another common story about performance at work links poor performance to 'lack of communication'.

Such analyses are interesting but limited:

People are Messy not Neat

Any individual has all sorts of motivations, varying from

- ➤ Moment to moment
- ➤ Day to day
- ➤ Week to week
- ➤ Year to year
- ➤ Life stage to life stage
- ➤ Place to place

Many motivations can be present at the same time. Variation within people is compounded by variation between people. Motivations themselves vary in strength and in the factors determining this strength. And of course motivation is not the only determinant of performance. Knowledge and skill level have a part to play!

Simple Theories Mean Few Levers

For example, if work functioning is entirely influenced by money then improving functioning means paying more money. No control over the money paid means no control over work functioning. A simple route to despair! If, however,

> motivations are more varied in their origin and content

> there are a range of other influences on performance and satisfaction

then a manager has more options available, more interventions to enhance staff functioning.

Reframing People at Work

To understand people at work requires a way of thinking that takes on board some of this complexity but that reduces it to manageable proportions. It needs a framework that helps the manager to identify

➤ The factors that promote and strengthen work relevant motivations
➤ The factors that undermine work relevant motivations
➤ The influence of additional factors such as knowledge and skill development on staff performance
➤ The factors that sustain or undermine good performance over time

This book uses a framework, known as the STAR model, to analyse the ways in which management action can

➤ Create and sustain the motivation to function well
➤ Ensure the competence to function well
➤ Sustain good functioning over time

THE STAR MODEL

The STAR model contains four elements.

1.   Setting Conditions

Setting conditions operate over varying periods of time and influence the strength of specific motivations. They influence the prominence and power of the wants and needs that a person experiences.

If a behaviour is understood as a means of escaping from a situation (the result), then setting conditions are factors which influence how threatened a person feels and why escape becomes so important.

If a behaviour is understood as a means of getting some form of stimulation (the result), then setting conditions are factors that make the desire for stimulation strong.

If a behaviour is understood as a means of gaining social status (the result), then setting conditions determine the strength of this desire for status.

The term setting conditions includes a wide variety of influences. Amongst the most important are

Past Experience

Learning history. A range of experiences influence current motivations:

An atmosphere where knowledge is valued and learning encouraged may build a long term wish to learn new information and skills.

The experience of continued rejection and being made to feel worthless may produce a strong craving for acceptance and a strong fear of criticism.

The repeated message that dependence on others is a sign of weakness will develop the desire for power and control over others and a fear of sharing and dependence.

Life events. Other kinds of experience are discrete events rather than general messages emerging from repeated specific experiences:

A serious loss such as a bereavement may lower mood, increase feelings of anger and rejection and strengthen the motivation to withdraw from social contact.

A traumatic event such as physical assault and abuse may increase feelings of anxiety and raise the likelihood of attack or escape (fight or flight) responses in a wide range of situations.

A series of daily hassles may increase tension and irritability and hence the need to remove these uncomfortable feelings.

Whilst a manager can exert no influence over an individual's past life and only a limited influence over their present life outside of work, the above does illustrate issues significant for the workplace.

➤   If a workplace offers the opportunity and encouragement to learn it may build the desire to learn
➤   If a workplace offers respect and value to individuals it will build confidence and the motivation to use initiative
➤   Emphasising team work and shared goals will build the wish to be part of the group
➤   Creating a safe environment will decrease the likelihood of anxiety based motivations entering work
➤   A significant organisational change will constitute a major life event and care will be needed during and after the change to reduce the likelihood of negative feelings and motivations

Thus an understanding of how experience shapes present functioning indicates ways of building motivations that support good quality human service work.

Social Climate

The quality of the current social relationships experienced by an individual will have an important influence upon wants and needs:

Active and continuing conflict between people will build tension and anger and the need to escape from/relieve these uncomfortable feelings.

Highly authoritarian relationships, with a clear and permanent distinction between those who control and those who are controlled, will raise frustration when individual needs are not met. They will also undermine belief in oneself as competent and thus the motivation to show initiative.

Good quality care services require staff to both work together and to show flexibility and initiative around the needs of individual service users. Given this, key management tasks will include

- ➤ Promoting harmony in staff relationships and effecting good conflict management
- ➤ Devolving decision making and promoting participation to the maximum degree possible

Physical Climate

Physical aspects of the environment will also affect the things that may be important for an individual at any one point in time.

Any source of discomfort in the working environment will increase the wish to escape from or avoid that environment.

Thus it becomes important to manage actively such factors as

- ➤ Noise level
- ➤ Temperature
- ➤ Illumination
- ➤ Odour
- ➤ Social density (crowding)

However, as well as influences from the past and current environments the structure of individual wants and needs may also reflect factors more 'internal' to the individual. These personal setting conditions include

Personal Health

The physical well being experienced by an individual will clearly influence the things that he/she seeks to achieve.

When in pain or other physical discomfort the most important thing becomes to achieve relief from this pain and discomfort. Other motivations will be reduced accordingly and general tolerance will decrease.

Whilst health is often seen as a personal matter employers are taking an increasing role in this area as the impact of health issues on work functioning and service quality is recognised.

The decisions about extending occupational health services lie outside the control of those to whom this book is addressed. However, some consideration of these issues will be given in the chapter on stress at work.

Personal Attitudes and Beliefs

Beliefs about oneself and interpretations of situations can influence motivations in a number of ways:

The belief that one must never make a mistake means that any situation where one does not get it right will be very threatening.

The belief that one must always be liked will make any form of criticism or rejection something to be avoided at all costs.

The belief that one must always be in control will provoke a strong response to anyone who disagrees or does not comply.

The belief in one's own ability to cope with problems influences persistence in the face of difficulties.

Given the long term, complex and uncertain nature of working with other people some beliefs and attitudes are more helpful than others. Management action can contribute to the promotion of constructive attitudes and beliefs in relation to the self.

Likewise in relation to attitudes and beliefs concerning those who use the services:

The belief that a user is inherently dangerous will promote anxiety and escape from/avoidance of the user.

The belief that a user is incapable of progressing will undermine the motivation to persist at helping the individual to gain skills or to access new experiences.

Attitudes and beliefs have an important and widespread role in determining the nature and strength of motivations . . . and they are accessible to change.

Emotional State

Human emotions are many, varied and ever changing. However, more sustained emotional states have important motivational implications:

Feelings of sadness will promote the wish to withdraw and to avoid social contact.

Feelings of anger will encourage the wish to 'take it out' on others.

Feelings of anxiety mean a need to escape from or avoid situations where this is experienced.

Feelings of enthusiasm will support innovation and persistence.

Feelings of happiness will improve responsiveness to all kinds of positive reinforcement.

A full consideration of the origins and determinants of these internal individual variables is beyond the scope of this book. However, anything that can be done in the workplace to develop and sustain personal

>   confidence
>   tolerance
>   well being

will support motivations relevant to good quality work in human services. Conversely
. . .

The concept of setting conditions is a wide one. It includes features of

>   the person
>   and the interaction between the two
>   the environment

Setting conditions influence the motivations that a person experiences and these in turn influence the behaviour of that individual. They 'set the scene' for Action (to use the STAR model term).

Clearly the creation of setting conditions which promote good quality work is a key area of management action. This book will describe a number of practical ways in which this can be done. However, setting conditions are not the only sources of motivation, and do not explain why an individual may choose

>   a particular course of action . . . at a particular moment in time

The STAR model includes a number of other factors which need to be considered.

2. *Triggers*

These are events (internal or external) that immediately precede action. They trigger behaviour. Triggers operate by

Reflex

A trigger may directly elicit a behaviour

A tap on the knee leads to a knee jerk.

An alarm clock leads to wakening.

A pull on the hair leads to a cry of pain.

This function is of limited value in terms of management action!

Priming Motivation

A trigger can influence the motivation experienced by the individual. It can create the motivation directly or may strengthen a motivation that is already present to some degree.

A noise such as screaming may create discomfort and the need for relief.

Sarcastic criticism from a manager may create anger in a staff member and if the staff member was already in an uptight state such anger will become the dominant motivation (as in 'the straw that breaks the camel's back').

A reminder about the importance and overall purpose of one's work may bring to the forefront social value motivations.

Recalling past successes and the goals to be achieved will strengthen the achievement motivations engaged by an item of work

Such priming of motivation is clearly a key area of management intervention. This will cover both

➤ Strengthening motivations that support good work
➤ Eliminating/reducing motivations that interfere with good work

Providing Information

A trigger can also indicate which particular behaviour is required and/or is likely to get one's needs met in a situation. This function of triggers operates in two ways.

a. Symbolic. Using the higher order systems that we have for conveying information:

Written programmes will indicate exactly how a job is to be done.

Timetables will indicate when and where jobs are to be done.

Written and spoken instructions, modelling and demonstration are all ways of directing behaviour not dependent upon direct experience of the actions in question.

b. Experiential. This aspect of triggering is based upon learning by experience. The trigger gains control over the action because the action when taken after the trigger is consistently associated with getting an important motivation satisfied:

If the presence of the manager is associated with interest in and encouragement for good quality work then this presence will in and of itself come to trigger such work in those to whom social approval is important

Likewise if this presence is associated with talking about such work then it will come to trigger the talking.

If a client consistently hurts others, then the presence of this client will come to trigger withdrawal

This information giving aspect of triggering is clearly another important area of management action in relation to staff performance. It includes

➤ Formal information systems such as timetables and written programmes
➤ Informal interactions such as the response of staff to particular user or manager behaviours

Although triggers serve rather different functions the thing that they have in common is that

> they occur close in time to behaviour and predict the fact that a behaviour is likely to occur

There are many controllable ways in which triggers can influence staff motivation and performance and these will be given consideration in subsequent chapters.

3. Actions

These are the behaviours that the individual carries out in order to satisfy salient wants and needs. They are the means of coping with the motivations experienced

➤ Achieving the desired positive outcomes
➤ Escaping from or avoiding important negative outcomes

In terms of this book the key actions are those that constitute good quality work. This requires

Defining Competence

Identifying the knowledge and skills that constitute good quality work in care services. This obvious point is all too often neglected.

Promoting Competence

Competence can be built in a number of ways. For example:

➤ Written materials
➤ Demonstration
➤ Instruction
➤ Feedback on practice

These inputs may occur

➤ Formally/informally
➤ In house/off site
➤ Individually/in groups

The concept of Actions indicates that people act to satisfy important wants and needs. If the actions of staff are not in line with quality performance it may be because they do not know how to function effectively

or because

the actions taken are more effective routes to meeting one's needs than the quality alternatives

Chatting to fellow staff members may be a more reliable route to social response and apprecia-tion than interaction with users who have major difficulties with communication and social responsiveness.

Thus Actions are intimately linked to the Results that they achieve. Equipping staff with the actions (knowledge and behaviours) that constitute good quality work is clearly an important area of management intervention. However, in itself it is unlikely to yield sustained performance unless attention is also given to that final element in the STAR model—Results.

4.   *Results*

These are the events that

follow Actions

and

influence whether particular Actions are repeated

Actions will continue in so far as they lead to the satisfaction of important motivations. Such satisfaction may be based upon

a.   Positive reinforcement. An Action is likely to be repeated in so far as it achieves something that the individual positively desires.

Demonstrable progress in client skills will sustain teaching efforts in someone who is achieve-ment oriented.

Praise for organising interesting activities will sustain this work in someone who is socially motivated.

Performance related pay will sustain targeted performance in those motivated by money, although the likely delay and inflexibility in the system will reduce its value as a means of influence.

A second form of satisfaction is based upon

b.   Negative reinforcement. An Action is likely to be repeated in so far as the individual escapes from or avoids unpleasant experiences.

Bawling a staff member out may get them away from the television and interacting with service users.

Patient calming and diffusion work with someone who is agitated will be sustained in so far as it reduces anxiety and avoids physical aggression.

Taking service users on outings will be sustained if it gets staff out of an unpleasant environment and tasks which do not succeed.

Whilst negative reinforcement is a common influence upon everyday human behaviour it has some problems in terms of its use in human service settings:

It requires the presence of something aversive for it to become effective.

Aversive experiences can increase anxiety or anger and thus breed motivations that are particularly counterproductive in this type of work.

It encourages avoidance learning.

One way of dealing with the 'critical' manager is to make sure you are not around when the manager is present. One way of dealing with the agitated client is to clear off and leave it to someone else.

Positive and negative reinforcement are processes that build up behaviours. However, behaviour may be influenced in the opposite direction. Current actions may be decreased by

c.   *Extinction.* An Action becomes less likely if it achieves nothing of importance to the individual.

Suggesting new ideas will be given up if the ideas are never considered or tried out.

Sustaining verbal interaction is difficult with someone who makes no discernible response.

Programmes that do not achieve the goals set will be hard to sustain.

Extinction is an important process to understand. It indicates the need to ensure that good performance achieves significant results . . . otherwise it will be extinguished. Human services commonly demonstrate large fluctuations in quality over time. Sustaining good quality practices has proved extremely difficult in relation to people with long term disabilities. Extinction may be one explanation of this—quality work may not achieve results significant for the staff. Another explanation may lie in the process of

d.   *Punishment.* An Action becomes less likely if it is consistently followed by something aversive.

Censuring staff for invading privacy of users will influence those who are socially motivated.

Ridiculing suggestions will discourage most people from making them.

Interaction will decrease when a user scratches anyone who goes near.

Whilst punishment can be a means of decreasing poor quality Actions by staff, its reliance on aversive interventions gives it similar problems to negative reinforcement. It will introduce anger and anxiety into situations where these motivations will be counterproductive.

It may produce avoidance of or aggression towards the source of punishment, be it manager or service user.

Of course any particular action may be subject to a number of different results and there may be a number of different actions that achieve similar results. One element of this complexity that it is important to understand is the process of

e. *Differential reinforcement.* Over time Actions will be shaped towards those that achieve the 'best' Results. Where one behaviour achieves better results than another more time will be spent on that behaviour.

Where managerial attention is focused more on writing reports than actually doing the job then socially motivated staff will allocate more time to writing.

When interacting with a group, more behaviour will be directed towards those who are more responsive.

If there is a choice between watching a favourite soap opera and helping someone who is very disabled or unmotivated to prepare tea then it is not hard to guess what might go on in the late afternoon.

Differential reinforcement is a very important process to understand particularly in relation to providing services to clients who are more disabled and disturbed. It indicates that good quality Actions must not only achieve important Results for the staff but must do so better than any other Actions available.

Maximising the Impact of Results on Actions

The effects of Results on Actions will be determined by a number of factors:

➤   The most influential Results are those that occur closest in time to an Action
➤   The influence of Results builds up through repeated experience
➤   Actions will sustain over long periods of time providing that Results are achieved intermittently. It is not necessary for an Action to 'succeed' every time.
➤   People vary between each other and over time as to what Results influence their behaviour. The important Results are those that link to and satisfy prominent motivations

Thus Results constitute a key area of management intervention. It is important that

➤   Good quality work achieves meaningful effects for staff
➤   Good quality work achieves a greater satisfaction of personal wants and needs than poor quality work
➤   The role of positive reinforcement is more prominent than that of negative reinforcement or punishment

CONCLUSIONS

The above describes the STAR framework for analysing the factors that influence work functioning. Table 2.1 summarises the elements in the framework and gives examples of their implications for management action. The book will be organised around this framework and will identify the practical steps that managers can take in order to

➤ Create and sustain the motivations of staff to do the job well
➤ Create and sustain high quality staff performance

Table 2.1 Examples of the STAR system applied to management action

STAR factors	Management action
Setting conditions	
Past experience	
learning history	Goal oriented work systems for staff and clients, strong staff development programme
life events	support work during/after organisational change
Social climate	Clear purpose for service and work group, participative decision making
Physical climate	Maintenance of decor
Personal health	Occupational health services
Personal attitudes and beliefs	Training for role, supervision
Emotional state	Maintain high levels of positive reinforcement, supervision, staff counselling service
Triggers	
Priming motivation	Reminders of work values, reminiscing about past successes
Providing information	Rules of conduct, programme plans, timetables
Actions	
Defining competence	Accurate job descriptions
Promoting competence	On the job coaching, training
Results	
Positive reinforcement	Formal and informal systems of positive feedback for competent performances
Negative reinforcement	Not recommended
Extinction	Ensuring that poor quality performances do not access positive reinforcement
Punishment	Constructive criticism after poor quality staff actions
Differential reinforcement	Ensuring that important positive reinforcements are more easily accessed by good as opposed to poor quality staff actions

Examples: the model in action

Vignette I

The Service

Dimview is a residential service for six people who are elderly and severely mentally infirm. It is late afternoon in the living room. Present are all the residents and two staff, Bill and Vera. The television is on. The shift leader is in a room that has been designated the staff room.

Setting Conditions

It is not clear to anyone what the Dimview service is trying to achieve. Some see it as just providing physical care, others see it as trying to improve the quality of life for the users. There are frequent arguments amongst the staff about this and other matters. There is no clear guidance from management but when the patch manager visits he tends to comment on the tidiness in the house and the cleanliness of residents.

There is some form of annual review for each user, attended by the manager, shift supervisors and the community social worker. Care staff do not attend but are occasionally told that they should be trying to get a particular user to do more for him/herself. Nobody follows up on this and nothing much gets done. There is in fact a high staff turnover at Dimview so that often staff on duty know little about the users and the work that is to be done with them.

Triggers . . . and Staff Actions

Suddenly Mr Arthur starts to scream, something he does quite often. It is a very piercing sound and tends to wind everyone up. Bill looks at his watch and mutters something about the washing cycle being finished and walks out of the room. 'Typical' thinks Vera and goes over to see what the problem is for Mr Arthur.

Results

At that moment the shift leader puts her head round the door and says 'What a racket . . . he's just being attention seeking, Vera . . . you're only encouraging him by fussing over him . . . go and make a cup of tea for us all, that should shut him up.' As she wandered back to the staff room she saw Bill in the peace and quiet of the laundry room. 'Thanks for sorting that out, Bill.'

Comment

The setting conditions do not create the motivations needed for relationship oriented, user centred work. This is compounded by the responses to the various staff actions. Vera is punished for interacting with the service user. Bill is reinforced for not interacting with the service user—the negative reinforcement achieved by leaving the room, the positive reinforcement from the supervisor for doing the laundry.

Vignette 2

The Service

Brightside is a residential service for six people who are elderly and severely mentally infirm. It is late afternoon in the living room. Present are five of the residents and two staff, Bill and Vera. The television is on. The shift leader is in the kitchen with one of the residents, making afternoon tea for everyone.

Setting Conditions

Brightside has a very clear policy of working actively to improve the quality of life for those who use the service. This features in written documents, is central to the staff induction process which all staff go through and is something formally reviewed once a year at a meeting of staff, management, users and relatives of users. Each user has an annual individual planning meeting and a monthly review of progress. Each user has a key worker amongst the staff and the annual planning meeting is attended by the key worker, the service manager, the community social worker and of course the individual concerned. All staff attend all monthly progress review meetings. The annual meeting designates goals for the year and progress on these is checked at the monthly meetings. The goals and progress reports are well documented. Sometimes disagreements arise amongst staff but these are discussed openly and usually resolved at the monthly meetings or the quarterly staff meeting. There is some turnover of staff but no more than about 15% per annum, with people mostly moving on to promotion or further training.

There is no separate staff area at Brightside and visits from the service manager usually focus on how individual users are getting on and how staff are feeling.

Triggers . . . and Staff Actions

Suddenly Mr Arthur starts to scream, something he does quite often. It is a very piercing sound and tends to wind everyone up. Bill looks over to Vera and they quickly decide who will attend to Mr Arthur. Vera in fact gets on well with him and so she takes it on. She goes over to check out the problem whilst Bill reassures the others present. The shift leader looks in to see if any help is needed but is reassured that matters are in hand.

Mr Arthur has no speech but after following his gestures and his response to some direct questions Vera understands that he is upset by the programme on TV, which is a war film set in London during the Blitz. Vera suggests that they go off to the dining room and do something else together and Mr Arthur indicates his agreement. Vera helps him up and assists him to walk to the dining room (he cannot walk unaided).

Results

Mr Arthur soon calms as he and Vera look through the pictures of a recent party. Tea arrives. Later in the afternoon the shift leader takes both Vera and Bill on one side and thanks them for dealing with the situation so sensitively.

Comment

The setting conditions create the motivations towards user centred work. These are channelled by systems of goal setting (triggers) and monitoring/feedback (results). These systems are supported by the informal interactions illustrated in the vignette. Vera and Bill are reinforced for their actions by both negative reinforcement (the screaming stops) and positive reinforcement (comments from the supervisor).

SUMMARY

1. QUALITY IN HUMAN SERVICES WORK REQUIRES ATTENTION TO BOTH JOB SATISFACTION AND JOB PERFORMANCE.

2. SATISFACTION AND PERFORMANCE DEPEND UPON MOTIVATION, INFORMATION, SKILL LEVEL AND THE RESULTS ACHIEVED BY ONE'S BEHAVIOUR.

3. THE STAR MODEL OFFERS A WAY OF ANALYSING THESE INFLUENCES.

4. THE STAR MODEL SEES FUNCTIONING AS DETERMINED BY SETTING CONDITIONS, TRIGGERS, ACTIONS AND RESULTS.

5. SETTING CONDITIONS ARE FACTORS OPERATING OVER TIME, WHICH INFLUENCE THE STRENGTH AND PROMINENCE OF MOTIVATIONS. THEY INCLUDE PAST EXPERIENCE, CURRENT SOCIAL CLIMATE, CURRENT PHYSICAL CLIMATE, PERSONAL HEALTH AND INTERNAL PSYCHOLOGICAL FACTORS.

6. TRIGGERS ARE EVENTS THAT IMMEDIATELY PRECEDE BEHAVIOUR AND THAT INFLUENCE IT BY REFLEX, BY PRIMING MOTIVATION AND BY PROVIDING INFORMATION.

7. ACTIONS REFER TO STAFF BEHAVIOUR AND TO ACHIEVE QUALITY IN WORK PERFORMANCE REQUIRES ATTENTION TO BOTH DEFINING AND PROMOTING COMPETENCE.

8. RESULTS ARE WHAT HAPPEN AFTER ACTIONS AND THAT DETERMINE WHETHER OR NOT ACTIONS WILL BE REPEATED. THEY OPERATE BY THE PROCESSES OF POSITIVE REINFORCEMENT, NEGATIVE REINFORCEMENT, EXTINCTION, PUNISHMENT AND DIFFERENTIAL REINFORCEMENT.

9. THE BOOK WILL USE THE STAR MODEL TO EXAMINE THE WAYS IN WHICH MANAGERS CAN CREATE AND SUSTAIN THE MOTIVATIONS OF STAFF TO WORK WELL; AND CREATE AND SUSTAIN ACTUAL QUALITY PERFORMANCE.

SECTION II

Creating and Sustaining Motivation

In terms of the STAR model, Chapters 3 to 7 deal with SETTING CONDITIONS.

> **Setting conditions operate over varying periods of time and influence the strength of specific motivations. They influence the prominence and power of the wants and needs that a person experiences . . and these in turn influence the behaviour of that individual . . .. The concept of setting conditions is a wide one. It includes features of the person,**

> **the environment and the interaction between the two . . .. They 'set the scene' for Action . . ..**

Chapter 8 deals with TRIGGERS in so far as these affect motivation

> **Triggers . . . are events (internal or external) that immediately precede action. They trigger behaviour. Triggers operate by**
>
> **Reflex . . . Priming motivation . . . Providing information**

Although triggers serve rather different functions the thing that they have in common is that they occur close in time to behaviour and predict the fact that a behaviour is likely to occur.

CHAPTER 3   What are we here for?

AIMS OF THE CHAPTER

1. To explain the nature and functions of a service mission statement.

2. To identify how to formulate, disseminate, sustain and review the service mission.

INTRODUCTION

There comes a time in any job when a staff member asks

'What am I doing this for?'
'Why am I putting up with this?'
'What on earth are we trying to achieve here?'

Such thoughts usually occur at times of stress or crisis. Unless these questions can be answered in a

realistic and personally meaningful way

then the motivation and performance of the individual is in jeopardy. Unless the answer has much in common with

the answers given to similar questions by other staff members, including managers

then the quality of the overall service is in jeopardy.
A clear and shared sense of purpose is an important source of

motivation and practical guidance

Its existence and its reinforcement in the hearts and minds of staff is a vital setting condition for any organisation concerned with quality. In particular

➤ It supports and mobilises such work relevant motivations as the wish to achieve social value and respect and the wish to experience efficacy and achievement
➤ It is a central aspect of team development and will ensure that the motivation to be part of a group is directed towards work relevant behaviour

An important way in which such a purpose is expressed is through a mission statement. A mission statement is more than a collection of words on a piece of paper, even though this might be one medium through which it is expressed. Mission statements should exist at all levels in an organisation:

- The total organisation
- Individual service elements
- Particular staff teams

The first section of this chapter will be concerned with the content aspect of a mission statement. Subsequent sections will focus on process elements—how to

> develop
> sustain
> bring alive
> keep under review

mission content.

MISSION STATEMENT CONTENT

This is summarised in Table 3.1. A mission statement outlines for a service:

1.   *Key goals.* Who the service is for and what it is trying to achieve for those who use the service

Examples

A service for people diagnosed as suffering from dementia to enable them to retain skills and knowledge for as long as possible and to experience respect irrespective of level of functioning.

A service for people with learning difficulties, between 16 and 25, to develop skills that enable them to function independently in an urban setting so that they might lead an ordinary life as part of the local community.

A service for people with chronic psychiatric illness that will enable them to achieve the maximum possible sense of personal well being and that enables them to develop personally in areas that they wish to develop in.

The goals should incorporate a long term visionary outcome and outcomes that are attainable given present resources.

2.   *Key methods of work.* Central aspects about how a service goes about achieving its goals, the 'tools of its trade'.

Examples

By the development of close and continuing personal relationships and the application of structured techniques for supporting learning and retention.

By the application of a broad and balanced curriculum and the development of individualised programmes of learning.

By a close examination of individual needs and a flexible approach to meeting those needs that are most related to personal well being. By offering a personal mentor relationship and continuing opportunity and choice.

3. *Key values.* The reasons why such goals and methods are given priority.

Examples

Everyone is entitled to respect no matter how they behave and is entitled to assistance to retain the maximum degree of independence possible.

Everyone should be helped to achieve their full potential, no matter what that potential is.

Suffering should be alleviated and different lifestyles respected provided that they do not infringe the rights of others.

The mission statement is thus focussed upon the central being of a service, the most important aspects of it. In brief

> it should be possible to state a mission in no more than a minute and write a statement no longer than ½–¾ page of A4 paper

The mission should be represented

> visually as well as verbally—a summary picture or logo

The mission is a blend of practical and inspirational content. It both guides and uplifts.

Table 3.1   Mission statement content

Key goals
Key work methods
Key values

Mission Statement or Operational Policy

A mission statement will form but one part of an operational policy. The two differ in

➤ Length
➤ Function
➤ Content

The mission is brief, primarily assisting motivation but also relevant to service evaluation. The operational policy is longer, primarily about setting standards and not really motivational. It is an administrative rather than a psychological tool.

Some Mission Related Difficulties in Care Services

A clear, shared and living sense of purpose is not something often found in services for those who deviate in our society. Common problems that arise include

No Mission

Most services have long operational policy documents

- ➤ Buried in folders and drawers
- ➤ Rarely referred to
- ➤ Largely unknown to staff

Most services have some individual staff members fired by a personal vision. In some cases such visions are shared by more than one staff member. But a widely shared view, living actively in hearts and minds, is a rare occurrence.

Default Mission

Some services have a shared view, rarely put into any formal document, that they are there to provide services for people that nobody else wants. This is a particular problem for services where a high proportion of users are very seriously disabled or disturbed. Such a mission reflects the despair often felt by providers in such settings. It offers

- ➤ No inspiration
- ➤ No direction
- ➤ No distinctive personally owned purpose

It sees the service as entirely determined by the whims of others—those that do the excluding. Without wishing to be receptaclist, it is hard to feel positive about being a dustbin. Such a default view actively damages rather than enhances motivation.

Mission Impossible

Some services have mission statements that are completely out of line with the resources available to a service so that it is impossible to achieve any of the designated goals.

Examples

A service with the goal of getting a group of people in wheelchairs to access the local community but which rarely has more than one staff on duty at any one time.

A mission stressing dignity and choice but a laundry system that means that people do not always wear their own clothes.

A service for helping those with behavioural and emotional difficulties run by staff untrained in this work.

This experience of being set completely unrealisable goals breeds

- ➤ Frustration
- ➤ Cynicism
- ➤ Alienation

It actively demotivates staff.

A mission statement must certainly have a visionary element, lifting heads to the far horizon. But it must also have an attainable element if disillusion is to be avoided.

The situations depicted above will lead to

➤ Demotivation of individuals and working groups through lack of purpose and value
➤ Conflicts between individuals or groups as different 'missions' are pursued.

Both these outcomes are incompatible with quality experiences for service users.

Thus a clear, shared and living mission has a critical role in the provision of care services. This section has defined what a mission is and why it is important. The next sections go on to examine the processes of

➤ Development
➤ Dissemination
➤ Renewal

DEVELOPING A MISSION STATEMENT

A mission statement can be developed in a number of ways and the discussion will outline some of these. It is not intended as a step by step guide to be followed rigorously—more as a collection of ideas to be adapted flexibly to 'local' circumstances.

The process of identifying a core mission is relevant to both

➤ An operational service in need of revitalisation
➤ A new service being planned

In the former case, where a service in operation has lost its way (or never had one), it will be important to resolve any outstanding major grievances before engaging in the process of mission development. Whilst there are prominent grievances these will dominate the motivations of service providers. This in turn will interfere with their

➤ Willingness to engage in activity to develop a mission
➤ Ability to respond to a mission that has been defined

Table 3.2 Developing a mission statement

Define the contributors
Canvass opinions
Formulate the mission
Draft the statement
Develop the visual symbol

The process of developing a mission will involve a number of activities, summarised in Table 3.2.

Define the Contributors

The active contributors will depend very much upon the organisational style and under-lying belief systems of the service.

At one extreme lies a service run by a 'charismatic' leader. She alone

➢   Defines what a service is about
➢   Ensures that everyone understands this
➢   Ensures that deviations are quickly picked up or prevented

Many pioneering services reflect this model. Such a leader will tend to attract/recruit 'disciples' so that the maintenance process is made easier. Thus the mission is

➢   Defined and embodied by a single individual
➢   Disseminated in a hierarchical, top down manner

The advantages of this approach are that

➢   It can lead to a very clear sense of purpose, with staff knowing exactly what the service is about and where they stand
➢   It reduces uncertainty and limits the responsibility of staff to doing the job, not also having to worry about what the job is

The vulnerabilities are that

➢   It is very dependent upon the individual personality and a service can lose its way very rapidly when the leader departs or becomes incapacitated
➢   It requires a degree of leadership stability which is hard to deliver in a secular world marked by job mobility
➢   It can reduce the level of commitment and ownership experienced by staff as it puts so many key decisions in the hands of a single individual
➢   Its identification of person and mission can lead to difficulties in accommodating new knowledge, new attitudes, new consumer needs and preferences. Such services can become inward looking and experience the phenomenon of 'groupthink' so that any dissent from the 'conventional' view is discouraged

This last point is particularly problematic in

➢   A society marked by rapid change
➢   Areas where knowledge is growing at a rapid pace

These are both characteristic of the field of long term disability in many societies. The 'leader decides' option thus has serious limitations as a generalised approach to develop-ing a mission statement.

At the other extreme of the 'contribution' spectrum lies extensive participation. This would see defining a purpose for a service as something that involves staff and consumers at every level.

In between these two extremes lie many intermediate options. The process might involve

➢   Representatives of interested parties
        or

➤ Managers only

or

➤ All those who provide services but not consumers

From a psychological perspective genuine participation in the process of defining the mission is a good means of securing understanding and commitment. Its advantages are that it can

➤ Enhance the motivation to work towards the goals set out in the mission by increasing the sense of ownership of the mission itself
➤ Spread more easily true understanding of the mission
➤ Make available a wider range of ideas at the stage of formulating the mission

However, the participation must be experienced as genuine. This means that

➤ The outcome or defined parts of it are seen to be negotiable
➤ People are able to express themselves freely
➤ Views are listened to with respect
➤ Conflicts are acknowledged and worked through skilfully

A participative approach requires a high degree of skill from whoever is managing the process if its benefits are to be realised. If the process is not handled skilfully (for example, if people find that the outcome has already been decided or if certain opinions are put down) then those involved will feel disillusioned and their motivation will be actively undermined.

The participative approach therefore has disadvantages

➤ It takes longer
➤ It requires a high level of interpersonal managerial skill
➤ If mishandled it will damage motivation

Thus defining the contributors and the scope for choice is a very important step. The advantages of a participative approach probably outweigh the disadvantages, from a motivational perspective. However, participation is not the only route to understanding and commitment.

Develop the Statement

Whoever is involved, the development process itself will go through a series of phases.

1. Initial Canvassing

Contributors formulate their personal views about the service mission. This might involve, singly or in combination

➤ Face to face discussions in one-off or a series of contributors' meetings
➤ Individual freehand written submissions
➤ An initial questionnaire to help focus the thinking of contributors.

People will need time to think about the issues involved and it is important not to compress this stage too much. The temptation to do all the work in a single time slot (the whole day meeting, the three day residential workshop) should be resisted. It can produce too strong a social pressure for agreement. The outcome will then reflect

> the social dynamics within the group

rather than

> the reality of the service

2.   Formulation

Once contributors have had time to

> consider the issues
> articulate their views on an individual basis

the time is right to move towards a shared definition of service mission. This will be the time for more intensive group work in order to

a.   Identify areas of general agreement.

b.   Check general agreements by clear definition of terms. This ensures that similar words mean similar things to people. People may use the same words (potential, respect, choice) but mean entirely different things. It is important to press contributors to describe in concrete terms what would be seen to be going on in a service that

> demonstrated respect
> offered choice
> used community resources

or whatever other terms are used. Only when it is clear that words used have a shared understanding should they be incorporated in to the statement.

c.   Identify areas of disagreement. Disagreement is inevitable and it is important that this is accepted, indeed encouraged. Diversity of view is a key to creativity and development if handled well. It can of course also be a destructive force.

d.   Resolve conflicts. The resolution process begins with an open discussion of the opinions and the reasons underlying them. The reasons behind opinions are vital to access as they often highlight areas of agreement underlying apparent disagreements.

Example

There may be an argument as to whether a service should be about engaging elderly people in a range of activities or offering peace and quiet, underlying which may be agreement on the importance of dignity, respect and maintaining functional capacities.

Identifying areas of underlying agreement may make it easier to resolve apparent conflicts.

If group work gets stuck so that issues are not progressed then the group needs first to articulate its decision rules should consensus fail to be achieved. Consensus is the ideal outcome but, if this seems impossible, group members must know how a decision will be made:

➤ 'Leader decides'
➤ Majority voting
➤ Referral to 'arbitration'

The fallback position must be known in advance. However, such an outcome can be avoided and the likelihood of consensus enhanced if the leader uses one or more of the specific interventions outlined in Table 3.3.

Table 3.3   Tactics for resolving conflicts and building consensus in group decision making

---

a.   *Call time out*—break the group so that participants can go away, reflect upon issues and then try again. This kind of break should be at least 24 hours.

b.   *Use circle checks*—each member of the group states in turn what her personal opinion is and why she holds that view. Each member must make a statement and no comment from the other group members is allowed on the individual statements. Once the check is complete discussion can continue. It serves as a pause for taking stock of where the group is at. Circle checks may be useful when

- the discussion is being dominated by a few individuals
- the leader senses that there may be more underlying agreement than is apparent from the discussion

c.   *Use adversarial subgroups*—set up a debate. The discussion group is divided into three

- those in favour of a point of view
- those against/in favour of an alternative view
- 'cross benchers'

With small groups just the two 'sides' may be adequate. Each group is made up of

- those who really hold a position
- those who do not (some people have to argue against their own position)

Each group is given a limited time to present its arguments and is then questioned. The whole group breaks (refreshment length); and then normal discussion resumes to see if now the group can resolve its differences.

d.   *Resymbolise*—up until now all the discussion has been verbal. It may help to resolve an issue if those holding a particular view are asked to produce a picture/visual representation of that view. Moving to a different medium of symbolisation may

- 'unstick' thinking
- illuminate important areas of agreement

It also foreshadows an important later process in mission formulation.

These tactics are likely to resolve any conflict within the group and enable consensus to be reached. Should resolution not occur then the group will use its known fallback decision rule.

3.   *Drafting the Mission Statement*

The ideas have been assembled and agreed. They now need to be summarised into a statement. This must be brief enough so that it

➤   Encourages people to read it
➤   Is likely to be remembered

A guide would be that the statement occupy no more than ½–¾ of a page of A4 paper.

4.   *Developing a Visual Symbol*

Once the statement is made it will be helpful to produce some visual symbol to support that statement. This may be a

➤   Representational picture
➤   More abstract symbol (logo)

It should be distinctive. Such symbols

➤   Are memorable
➤   Are readily disseminable (see below)
➤   Give a very clear sense of being special and discriminable as a service

The development of a clear sense of purpose will be a process of direct help to those involved. It will engage the motivations outlined earlier. However, the function of a mission is to broaden that engagement to all service providers now and over time. Thus disseminating and sustaining the mission is the real key to realising its motivational potential.

DISSEMINATING AND SUSTAINING THE MISSION

This involves a wide variety of activities, summarised in Table 3.4

Table 3.4   Disseminating and sustaining the mission

Circulate the statement widely
Present the statement at all formal meetings
Use the visual symbol on a widespread and 'unexpected' basis
Make available indirectly supportive materials
Remove non-supportive materials
Refer to mission during decision making
Use mission as part of motivational briefings
Refer to mission in any feedback on staff performance
Put the mission at the centre of induction for new staff

Spread the Word

The statement itself should be circulated to all those involved in providing service. It should be formally presented

to all meetings
at all levels

within the organisation.

Get the Picture

The visual symbol should always accompany the written/spoken presentation of the mission. However, the beauty of the picture is that it can be presented in all sorts of situations not accessible to the written word. Once the association has been formed it can be used to evoke the sense of purpose. Traditionally such symbols find their way on to

➤ Letterheads
➤ Other forms of standard documentation

This is important but people do habituate to this and the impact of the symbol is likely to decrease over time. This can be counteracted by introducing the symbol on a temporary and unexpected basis so that

attention is caught and the mission evoked

Example

One group decided to stamp the logo on to pay slips . . . every so often.
Stickers and stamps make such graffiti readily possible and introduce a surprise, perhaps even a fun (!), element.

Get the Message

Sometimes it is possible to support the key messages in a mission statement more indirectly. This can be surprisingly effective and indicates the importance of considering some of the less obvious elements in a service environment.

Examples

If a key message of the service is understanding and respect rather than imposition and control then availability of *National Geographic* magazine is more supportive than a boxing magazine, to put it in an extreme way.

An emphasis on rights is better supported by the presence of Amnesty International materials than by posters of performing dolphins.

An emphasis on struggling to make progress in the face of complex problems and limited resources is better supported by material on intermediate technology than it is by information on high technology.

There should be careful consideration of the messages primed by materials casually available in a service environment. Such indirect routes are an important source of support (or otherwise) to more direct information transmission.

Remember . . . Remember

For the mission to come alive it must be referred to frequently. Examples include

a.   *When decisions are being made about service plans for an individual.*

b.   *When a crisis arises and decisions are needed.* For example

➤   An individual service user behaving in a very disturbed fashion
➤   A resource crisis within a service

It is at these points that decisions based upon short term expediency can be made. Such decisions can

➤   Undermine a service's purpose
➤   Destroy belief in the mission

The damage to motivation may extend well beyond the crisis period.

c.   *During prospective briefings.* The time when staff may be together before or between shifts may be a time to remind them of

➤   What the service stands for
➤   How this relates to the work period that they are about to undertake

Briefings are often used just to convey immediate, day to day information. Sports coaches are well aware of the importance of 'psyching up' prior to an event. This goes beyond the mechanics of specific movements and tactics and includes an element that relates to

the broader purpose of what they are doing and why

This is an approach which can be adapted to many human service situations. It moves the mission statement from a background setting condition to a motivational trigger.

d.   *When giving feedback about work done.* Reference to the mission will be an important part of both positive feedback and constructive criticism.

The first thing you need to know is . . .

The mission is the heart of the service, its core element. As such it should feature prominently in both

staff selection
and
staff induction

procedures. It is essential that new staff or potential new staff have a full understanding of what the service

➤ Stands for
➤ Is striving for

This is not just having to read the statement but being actively involved in discussing, questioning and looking at how the service does and does not fulfil its mission.

Example

Get new or prospective staff to spend time accompanying a service user and trying to experience the service from the user's perspective. This experience can then be reviewed in the light of the expressed mission. This will promote genuine understanding of the service and its mission.

Establishing a mission in the hearts and minds of providers is not a once and for all activity. A mission needs to be reviewed.

REVIEWING THE MISSION

All services should engage in periodic review, quite separate from ongoing monitoring of service quality. A service is not a static element isolated from the outside world. It is part of a bigger system and both influences that system and is influenced by it. Every so often there is a need to step back and review what is going on. This is the chance to reaffirm or change the mission.

The mechanisms will vary but a number of key elements will be present.

1.   Review will take place in a designated but limited time period—some services may take a day/two days out to do this, others set up a consultation process to take place within a defined period of time. It should occur every one to two years.
2.   The focus will be on longer term issues, not day to day matters except in so far as those reflect the longer term issues.
3.   Participation will be extensive (see earlier discussion).
4.   There will be a definite outcome to the process:
    −   a reaffirming statement, or
    −   a statement of new purposes

The failure to take on board reflective review underlies many of the difficulties experienced by care services in sustaining quality. In our experience services may start off delivering high quality but lose their way. This may relate to

➤ Internal changes such as staff changes that lead to an unacknowledged redefinition of what a service is about
➤ Changes in the external environment

Example

We have worked in a number of educational settings where the initial aim was to teach children who were slow to learn, but generally well adjusted, a wide range of academic and practical skills.

Over time pupils applying to the school have much greater degrees of learning difficulty and higher levels of behavioural and emotional disturbance. Through a gradual, sometimes imperceptible, process an ever increasing proportion of the pupils are hard to teach and actively disturbed. There comes a point when it is clear that the service can no longer deliver what it thinks that it should be delivering. The service then drifts without a sense of purpose and quality can decline very rapidly.

Proactive intervention is vital to prevent this kind of scenario and drift can be forestalled with a planned system of service review.

CONCLUSIONS

A living mission is an important setting condition for priming and engaging some of the motivations that will sustain good quality work. These motivations include those related to achievement, those related to group membership and more altruistic motivations linked to important personal values. Maximising this motivational value requires planned and active processes to develop, disseminate, sustain and review the mission for a service. It is a necessary but not sufficient condition for initial and sustained service quality.

SUMMARY

1. A CLEAR AND SHARED SENSE OF PURPOSE (A SERVICE 'MISSION') IS AN IMPORTANT SETTING CONDITION FOR SUPPORTING AND PRIMING STAFF MOTIVATIONS, PARTICULARLY THOSE RELATED TO SOCIAL VALUE AND GOAL ATTAINMENT.

2. A MISSION STATEMENT CONTAINS KEY SERVICE GOALS, KEY WORKING METHODS AND KEY UNDERLYING VALUES.

3. THERE SHOULD BE SOME DEGREE OF PARTICIPATION BY MANAGERS, STAFF AND CONSUMERS IN THE PROCESS OF FORMULATING A MISSION.

4. THE PROCESS OF FORMULATION REQUIRES LEADERSHIP SKILLED IN FACILITATING PARTICIPATIVE PROBLEM SOLVING.

5. A MISSION STATEMENT SHOULD BE REPRESENTED IN WORDS (NO MORE THAN $\frac{1}{2}$–$\frac{3}{4}$ OF A PAGE OF A4) AND BY A VISUAL SYMBOL.

6. A RANGE OF TACTICS CAN BE USED TO DISSEMINATE AND KEEP ALIVE THE MISSION. BOTH DIRECT AND INDIRECT METHODS CAN BE USED. THE MISSION SHOULD FEATURE OFTEN IN THE DAY TO DAY LIFE AND DECISIONS OF A SERVICE.

7. ALL SERVICES SHOULD REVIEW THEIR MISSION AT LEAST ONCE EVERY TWO YEARS. THIS MAY LEAD TO REAFFIRMATION OR TO CHANGE IN THE LIGHT OF NEW KNOWLEDGE OR NEW DEMANDS ON A SERVICE.

Manager's toolkit	
Tools	Applications
Group discussions	Develop and review mission
Group conflict management	Mission development and review
Staff questionnaires	Canvas opinion on mission
Staff competition	Develop logo
Presentation to groups	Disseminate mission
Tracking users	Understand and reflect on mission
Multimedia communication	Reinforce mission
Psych-up briefings	Reinforce mission
Performance feedback	Reinforce mission

CHAPTER 4   What's it got to do with me?

AIMS OF THE CHAPTER

1. TO EXPLAIN THE IMPORTANCE OF FEELING THAT ONE'S VIEWS AND EFFORTS MAKE A DIFFERENCE ('PERCEIVED SELF EFFICACY').

2. TO DETAIL HOW TO ENHANCE MOTIVATION BY PARTICIPATIVE DECISION MAKING AND BY MANAGING THE LINK MADE BETWEEN PERSONAL EFFORT AND CHANGES THAT OCCUR ('ATTRIBUTION').

INTRODUCTION

The previous chapter introduced the idea that

> level of commitment at work is related to the level of involvement in decision making

This was discussed in relation to getting staff involved in the formulation and review of the service mission.

The present chapter broadens consideration of this topic. If people feel that by their own actions they are able to influence what goes on then they are

➤ More motivated to act . . . in general
➤ More likely to follow through on specific action plans
➤ More persistent in working on problems for which an immediate solution is not found

If on the other hand people believe that

> what they do makes no difference
> what happens is controlled by others
> what happens is determined by factors such as chance or luck

then they are less motivated to make an effort and to persist in the face of difficulties.

Working with people whose needs are long term and difficult to understand requires

➤ Initiative
➤ Ingenuity
➤ Persistence

Thus creating a work environment which fosters in staff the idea that they are effective constitutes an important setting condition.

Two ways of building this sense of personal effectiveness will be considered:

1. Giving staff influence over the goals and methods of work with service users (PARTI-CIPATIVE DECISION MAKING).
2. Strengthening the links made by staff between their personal efforts and positive outcomes for the service and its users, and reducing negative perceptions of users and colleagues (ATTRIBUTION MANAGEMENT).

PARTICIPATIVE DECISION MAKING

Why a Participative Approach

There are a number of advantages to getting staff actively and extensively involved in the decisions that affect them at work:

➤ Staff will feel greater ownership of these decisions and be more motivated to implement them without close or constant supervision

➤ Participation will be a means for staff of experiencing value and respect, thus enhancing work satisfaction and the likelihood of sticking with the job

➤ Participation can lead to better quality decisions because groups can generate more ideas than an individual working alone. This will be particularly important with problems for which there is no obvious 'right' answer

➤ Participation can lead to better quality decisions because staff may have information not available to a manager (such as detailed knowledge about an individual service user)

➤ A participative approach can open out disagreements and conflicts, thus making them accessible to change as opposed to remaining a source of tension

➤ A participative approach can generate a more general openness to change and innovation by reducing the number of standard procedures and accustoming staff to open communication and experimentation

However, there are negative aspects to a participative approach:

➤ Decisions may take longer
➤ Groups can become very set in their ways and not be very imaginative in their approach to problems ('groupthink')
➤ Participation can be very uncomfortable as it requires open, direct communication, something that many people are not accustomed to
➤ Participation takes effort and is harder work all round than a directive approach
➤ Participation requires a high level of competence in communication and other interpersonal skills. Such competence is required of both staff and managers and is not automatically present in people

Maximising the benefits and minimising the costs requires consideration of

➤ The type of decision best suited to a participative approach

➤   The organisational and individual prerequisites for successful participation
➤   The specific managerial skills for effecting participation

When to Use a Participative Approach?

The decisions best suited to a participative approach are those where

➤   There is no clear right/wrong answer
➤   Staff hold important information not available to the manager
➤   Staff need to implement the decision
➤   There is limited on the job supervision of staff
➤   The problems are complex and persistence will be required
➤   Acceptance of the decision is unlikely without participation

The more of these factors that are present the greater the need for a participative approach. Table 4.1 illustrates some examples of work practice decisions that reflect the need for high or low participation.

Many of the decisions that influence the quality of work in human services are such as to require a high level of involvement from staff in the decision making process.

Table 4.1   Examples of work practice decisions related to level of participation

Low level	High level
Stimulating swallow reflex	Helping a user make choices
Administering rectal Valium in case of extended seizures	Increasing opportunities for communication
Resuscitation in case of cardiac arrest	Finding ways for a user to express anger in a socially acceptable way
Staff duty rotas	Choosing a staff–user holiday

Organisational Prerequisites for a Participative Approach

Whilst involvement of staff in decision making has much to recommend it the organisation as a whole has to be adapted to this approach. Important prerequisites include

Shared Goals and Values

The work described in the previous chapter is an essential prerequisite for successful involvement. Without a clear, shared mission

➤   It will be hard to reach agreed decisions on a consistent basis
➤   People will pursue different agendas

Which means that

➤ High levels of participation will be accompanied by high levels of conflict and subsequent demotivation.

Decision Making Structures

Participative decision making

➤ Takes time
➤ Requires people to discuss together decisions to be made

This inevitably means withdrawing staff from direct work with users for periods of work time. Participation cannot occur

➤ Without a forum
➤ Without adequate time

The organisation has to allocate the necessary time and to develop a system of joint discussion and decision making. The pay off comes in terms of quality of face to face work resulting from this reduction in quantity.

A Culture of Participation

This is a much vaguer concept. The point to be stressed is that to get maximum motivational value from participation it needs to be seen as

more than a specific tool to be brought out on specific occasions

For staff to experience respect and value, the organisation as a whole needs to be seeking

➤ Every opportunity to increase participation and delegation
➤ Diverse methods to increase level of involvement

It would of course be ludicrous to suggest that all decisions can be handed over to staff providing the face to face care. However, in a culture of participation the emphasis is shifted to justifying non-delegation rather than having to justify delegation.

Supportive Selection and Training Procedures

The organisation needs to take on board the competence implications of a participative approach:

➤ The competence required of individual staff
➤ The competence required of the person managing the process of decision making (see below)

This will have implications for both selection and training procedures.

Individual Prerequisites of a Participative Approach

Topic Competence

Those involved in a decision must have some competence in relation to the issue under consideration.

It is no good asking someone who knows nothing about autism to be involved in developing an action plan for helping a person with autism to limit his obsessional behaviours within acceptable bounds.

It is no good asking someone who knows nothing about communication disorders to decide upon an approach to developing communication for someone suffering such a disorder

Work in care services involves three important areas of competence:

1. Detailed knowledge of the individual
2. General knowledge about human behaviour and its determinants
3. Specialised knowledge about the specific impairments and disabilities that an individual experiences

In any decision about work with an individual user all three areas of competence must be represented. Not everyone needs to be equally competent in all areas. But if an individual lacks competence in all areas then he/she can contribute little to decision making.

Communicative Competence

Participation requires a high level of COMMUNICATION and SOCIAL INTERACTION skills.

Staff need to be

➤ Willing and able to express their own point of view
➤ Willing and able to listen to the views of others

The manager needs to be

➤ Able to guide an individual staff member or a staff group through an issue to a decision

More details on these managerial skills are given below.

Levels of Participation

There are many ways in which staff can influence what goes on at work. Three important approaches are

Consultation

The manager shares an issue with staff and listens carefully to their views and then makes the decision.

Joint Problem Solving

The manager joins with the staff and together they work through a problem and reach an agreed decision. The manager has the key responsibility for guiding the problem solving process.

Delegation

The manager gives a problem to the staff and allows them to decide how it is to be resolved, agreeing thereby to abide by whatever decision is reached.

All these are helpful ways of involving staff and fostering motivation; and all are relevant in different situations. The key point is that whatever approach is used

➤ It should be genuine
➤ Staff should be clear about which approach is being used so that there is a shared understanding of how the decision will be made

The experience of genuineness comes from

➤ Being listened to with respect
➤ Experiencing over time that staff's views do influence decisions made even if one's own personal point of view does not win the day on a specific occasion

If participation is seen as a sham—for example:

if it is clear that decisions have already been made
if participation becomes bullying people into agreeing with the manager

then this will breed cynicism, lack of ownership and demotivation.

Because joint problem solving is the approach best suited to many of the key areas of client work and because it requires the greatest level of skill from the manager it will be the focus of more detailed consideration.

Effecting Joint Problem Solving

Joint problem solving can be described in terms of a series of stages each of which require skills from the person managing the process. These are summarised in Table 4.2.

Stage 1.   Define the Issue to be Decided Upon

If a decision is to be made, it is important to ensure that the issue is clear and any important constraints acknowledged. This will ensure that decisions made are concrete and realistic, which in turn raises the likelihood of successful implementation and the experience of personal effectiveness.

Table 4.2 Stages and skills in a joint problem solving approach

1. Define the issue to be decided upon
    Skills: stating, questioning, listening, summarising

2. Gather information on the issue
    Skills: questioning, listening, summarising

3. Identify the options for action
    Skills: questioning, listening/recording, brainstorming

4. Evaluate the options identified
    Skills: questioning, listening/recording

5. Elicit a personal statement about the preferred course of action
    Skills: questioning/listening, assertiveness

6. Reach a decision
    Skills: questioning/listening, conflict management

7. Translate decisions into tasks and responsibilities
    Skills: clear thinking, assertiveness

Manager skills:

➤ Stating—giving one's own understanding of the issue
➤ Questioning—drawing out from others their understanding of the issue
➤ Listening—to the views of staff about the issue
➤ Summarising—formulating the issue to be decided upon, the more concrete the statement, the easier it will be to decide on an action plan

It will be easier to decide on a programme to decrease the throwing of food than on a programme to decrease 'disruptiveness', a term which might cover many different issues and mean different things to different people.

Stage 2. *Gather Information on the Issue*

This means bringing out all that is known about the situation to be resolved. It is important at this stage

➤ To keep the focus on facts rather than speculations
➤ To draw in as many people as possible (if working with a group)

Example

When discussing what to do about a user's aggressive behaviour the emphasis initially is on what the user actually does, when it is most and least likely to occur, historical information and information about the user's current situation and well being rather than personal views about causation.

When discussing a leisure programme it will be important to focus on the known preferences of users and the resources likely to be available.

Manager skills:

- ➤ Questioning—moving initially from open ended questions to more closed questions in order to pinpoint information more precisely
- ➤ Listening—to the information given and views expressed
- ➤ Summarising—of the information obtained as a prelude to moving on

Stage 3.   *Identify the Options for action*

Before a decision is considered it will be useful to draw from those involved a range of possible ways of dealing with the situation. If the decision is about changing a currently problematic situation it will be important to draw out views as to why this situation exists (why a service user is behaving aggressively, why users are sometimes ending up wearing clothes that are not theirs).

Manager skills:

- ➤ Questioning—trying to ensure that everyone present gets involved
- ➤ Listening/recording—it may be helpful to note action ideas on a large sheet of paper that all present can view
- ➤ Brainstorming—give those involved a very short period of time (no more than a couple of minutes) to generate as many ideas as possible, even 'wild' ones, with no comment or evaluation on those ideas

Brainstorming is a way of

- ➤ Increasing the number of options
- ➤ Breaking up traditional thinking on issues
- ➤ Stimulating creativity

It is usually helpful to warm up to this with one or two practices on problems not related to the issues at hand.

Stage 4.   *Evaluate the Options Identified*

The ideas generated in Stage 3 are subject to evaluation in terms of pros and cons, benefits and costs. Everyone is involved in this and pressure to make a decision is resisted until this stage is completed.

Manager skills:

- ➤ Questioning
- ➤ Listening/recording—again it may be helpful to put on to paper all the pros and cons for each option

Stage 5.   *Elicit a Personal Statement about the Preferred Course of Action*

Use of the circle check technique will be helpful at this stage if the decision is being made in a group context. Each group member is asked to state

➤ His preferred action plan
➤ The reasons for this choice

No comments from other group members are allowed and no discussion occurs until everyone has had a say. This

➤ Ensures maximum involvement
➤ Counteracts the dominance of groups by more assertive members

Manager skills:

➤ Questioning/listening—whether or not the circle check technique is used
➤ Assertiveness—to control group members who wish to interrupt or comment

Stage 6.   Reach a Decision

It is important that all involved understand the decision making rules that operate. They must know whether decisions are made by

➤ Consensus
➤ Majority voting
➤ The group leader alone with the previous stages as a means of consultation only
➤ Some combination of the above (for example by consensus but with the leader retaining a veto)

Consensus is often preferred as a means of maximising ownership of a decision and hence the motivation to see the action plan through. However, more important than the rule itself is the fact that all those involved need to understand the rule. There is nothing more demotivating for staff than to think that they have control over a decision only to find it vetoed or denied. It is the misunderstanding of the decision making rule rather than the veto itself which is demotivating.

Manager skills:

➤ Questioning/listening—keeping everyone involved
➤ Conflict management—for continuing disagreements. Some procedures were discussed in the previous chapter. These included
  – getting people to articulate the reasons underlying their decisions
  – organising a 'cooling off' period
  – setting up adversarial subgroups

Stage 7.   Translate Decisions into Tasks and Responsibilities

The participative 'style' is a setting condition to enhance motivation. However, actual performance can be aided by a little triggering. The decision needs to be

translated into specific tasks
allocated to named individuals

This is particularly important in a group decision making context where it is all too easy to assume that someone else will actually carry out the decision—all too often everybody's responsibility becomes nobody's.

Manager skills:

➤ Clear thinking—so that tasks are analysed and the decision is put into concrete action steps
➤ Assertiveness—so that individuals know exactly what is expected of them

The above represents an idealised way of making decisions in a participative way. Not all discussions are likely to move in such a neat step by step fashion. However, it does serve to illustrate how an important, high sounding ideal such as 'participation' can be translated in to actual working practices.

Blocks to a Participative Approach

Whilst participation may be seen as a 'good thing' in theory, there can be many blocks to it occurring in practice. Common blocks include

➤ Lack of shared values and goals ('mission')
➤ Lack of competence in relation to the specific problem to be resolved
➤ Lack of the social skills needed to participate and/or to manage the process of participation
➤ Fundamental conflicts between individuals or groups of staff
➤ Time not allocated to decision making
➤ A previous history of non-participation breeding a resistance to any change in the status quo

The action needed to remove these blocks will vary:

➤ Time and perseverance will overcome resistance to change
➤ Training will help with job competence and social skill difficulties
➤ Management action can overcome conflicts and 'mission' difficulties

It is the view of this book that the time and effort needed to remove these blocks will be more than compensated by the positive outcomes that a participative approach yields. It may be tempting in the short run to make decisions for staff and to direct them in what is to be done. This may be perfectly appropriate in some work situations. However, in services where

quality (and equality) of relationships is central

great ingenuity, initiative and perseverance are required

A highly directive approach is disastrous.

MANAGING ATTRIBUTIONS

If staff perceive no link between

the efforts that they make at work

and

the outcomes in terms of working practices and client functioning

then there will be little job satisfaction and little motivation to solve and persist at problems.

If staff perceive their contribution as negative—as actually making things worse—then motivation and performance will be damaged.

If staff perceive service users as hostile, malevolent or beyond influence then it will be difficult to construct and sustain a close working relationship based upon

> Respect
> Unconditional positive regard
> Developmental expectations

Note that the issue here is how staff perceive and interpret things that go on at work. Their perceptions may or may not be 'true'.

The processes by which staff come to ascribe these relationships are clearly important to motivation and to longer term work performance. Four particular difficulties occur.

1. A positive change occurs (a client improves) but the change is not noticed.
2. A positive change is noticed but it is attributed to a factor that has nothing to do with staff—for example, to
   – the weather
   – the drugs prescribed by the doctor
   – the work of some other specialist
   – the passage of time
3. A negative change occurs and it is attributed to the staff—for example, staff are blamed for an aggressive incident.
4. A change occurs and it is attributed to a negative characteristic of the user—for example, aggression is attributed to a personal characteristic such as spitefulness or manipulativeness.

The issues to consider here are

> The accuracy of attributions
> The tendency to be problem focussed

Attribution Accuracy

Errors in interpretation of ourselves and other people can arise from a number of sources:

Lack of Information

We may simply lack information about a situation and make an error of judgement.

Example

Walking in on a situation where a user is acting in a disturbed way may be seen as an example of their mental illness unless we know that they have just heard about the death of a close friend

Prior Labelling

If a service user has been labelled by others in a negative way then this will encourage unhelpful views of their current functioning.

Examples

If an individual is labelled autistic then any strong personal interest that they have is likely to be called obsessional.

If an individual is labelled as a psychopath then any negative act will be seen as due to inherent lack of conscience as opposed to misunderstanding or genuine upset.

Hidden Beliefs

Sometimes the interpretations that people make reflect beliefs about themselves or about others that are hidden below the surface.

Examples

If a staff member had an upbringing which constantly reinforced the message that he/she was an incompetent, useless individual then it will be hard for that individual to see him/herself as achieving anything—any positive change is going to be attributed to factors other than personal skill or effort.

If a staff member believes that the process of Alzheimer's disease runs its own course without any possible influence then any changes will be seen as part of the disease process and not as reflecting the role of the environment.

If a staff member holds a view that people with learning difficulties are inherently violent and promiscuous then any expression of sexuality will be seen as threatening.

Emotional State

Emotional states tend to bias the processing of information.

Examples

If staff are very anxious then they will be more likely to interpret the behaviour of others as

- hostile
- threatening

If staff are depressed then they are more likely to

- see the behaviour of others as personally rejecting
- attribute positive changes to influences other than their own efforts
- blame themselves for negative occurrences

Problem Focussing

Human services do tend to be problem focussed and concentrate on things that are not going right rather than on those that are. A constant focus on negative aspects of a service user or a service will distort perceptions of both.

Specific Approaches to Positive Attribution Management

There are many ways of counteracting the interpretation difficulties outlined above. These are detailed below and summarised in Table 4.3.

Table 4.3   Positive approaches to attribution management

1. Strengths focussing
2. Descriptive orientation
3. Augment positive feedback
4. Reinforce helpful attributions
5. Challenge unhelpful attributions
   a. Provide correlational feedback
   b. Enrich the information field
   c. Encourage mini 'experiments'
   d. Probe for hidden beliefs
6. Support staff to overcome their emotional difficulties

Strengths Focussing

A general orientation to assess and rehearse the strengths of

    a user
    a service

as part of any problem solving process will help maintain a balanced view.

Descriptive Orientation

Great care is needed in the language used to describe clients and services. Language should be as

> objective

and

> descriptive

as possible. Negatively evaluative terms and labels with common negative connotations should be avoided.

Example

There is a big difference between calling someone a manipulative psychopath and saying that the person has difficulty sustaining relationships and managing anger.

Augment Positive Feedback

In work with people who have serious, long term disabilities progress is likely to be slow and variable. It is vital that positive changes that do occur, no matter how small, are noted and amplified. It is important to

- Comment verbally on changes
- Use graphs and charts to illustrate changes over time
- Challenge staff to think back to the situation at an earlier time (say, some months ago) and recall any differences between then and now

Reinforce Helpful Attributions

If staff make useful links between their efforts and what is achieved these should be encouraged by agreement and repetition.

Challenge Unhelpful Attributions

It is important for attributions to be accurate. This may mean facing the fact that some of our efforts have no impact and some make things worse. However, as outlined above attributions are error prone and it will be helpful to challenge unhelpful attributions even if in the end they turn out to be accurate.

Challenging can be done in a number of ways:

a.   Provide correlational feedback. Making a clear link between the timing of staff efforts and a positive change will help develop the attribution linking one to the other. This can be done by

> ➤ Getting staff to recall the sequence of events
> ➤ Using charts which show both the client changes and changes in staff input
> ➤ Allocating tasks to specific individuals

Example

Linking an improvement in the mood of a user to the staff's efforts to provide a more pleasurable lifestyle will cut across the tendency to see the mood change as something controlled entirely from within.

b.   Enrich the information field. Correlational feedback is one way of increasing the information on which to base attributions. There are a number of others:

> ➤ Challenging the way staff are interpreting events may enable them to think differently
> ➤ Getting staff to identify and monitor positive aspects of a user (good/successful things that they do) will help to challenge negative attitudes towards a user
> ➤ Getting staff to assess situations in more detail may alter interpretations

Example

Finding out that a client's behaviour difficulties occur in a range of situations will challenge the interpretation that 'it's only with us and therefore we must be to blame'.

c.   Encourage mini 'experiments'. Change is always threatening. Getting staff to try out in a very limited way different approaches to a situation and monitoring the effects that the variations have is a way of influencing interpretations.

Example

A teacher faced with a 'hyperactive' child who would not settle to activities looked at different ways of presenting activities. On some sessions she actively prompted the child to work on activities and on others she waited until he approached an activity and then worked with him. She monitored how much time he spent on a task. By waiting until he approached she found that she got much more work out of him. This not only informed her as to how best to meet his needs but showed that although he was labelled 'hyperactive' he was very much influenced by how staff related to him.

d. *Probe for hidden beliefs.* Careful but sustained questioning about why staff are interpreting a situation in the way that they are may get down to the kinds of hidden beliefs outlined above. These are likely to be beliefs about which the individual

➤ Is not fully aware
➤ May feel uncomfortable

Thus great care needs to be taken in opening them up. However, once people become aware of them it makes the beliefs amenable to change.

Example

Working with a parent of a child with learning difficulties who had frequent temper tantrums it became clear that the best approach would be to allow the child to calm down in peace and quiet rather than trying to intervene in any more active way. The parent readily agreed to this but found in practice that he could not do it. A number of reasons were given but on probing it emerged that the parent believed that if the child got upset at all it would trigger epileptic seizures. Once this was clarified the issue was investigated and once reassured the parent was able to follow through on the programme.

The aim of these efforts is not to deceive staff or to produce a false but helpful set of attributions. Rather it is to check erroneous and unhelpful attributions which undermine motivation.

Support Staff to Overcome their Emotional Difficulties

Skilled support will

➤ Enhance personal well being
➤ Reduce the attribution biases outlined above

The subject of staff stress will be looked at more closely in Chapters 15 and 16. However, it is important to recognise that

work with people who have long term, severe difficulties

and

for whom it is a continual challenge both to understand and to meet their needs

is extremely stressful. The stress levels are likely to be reflected in the sorts of attributions that staff make. Such attributions add further to the motivational damage created by the prolonged stress itself.

CONCLUSIONS

Developing a sense of personal effectiveness is vital to staff motivation and performance. This can be done by increasing the amount of control staff have over their working lives and by maximising the positive links that staff make between their efforts and what is achieved. This is effected by creating a culture of participation and self awareness; and by very specific management interventions.

SUMMARY

1. THE NATURE OF WORK IN CARE SERVICES MEANS THAT IT IS VITAL TO CREATE THE CONDITIONS WHEREBY STAFF FEEL THAT THEY CAN INFLUENCE WORK PROCESSES AND OUTCOMES FOR SERVICE USERS.

2. TWO WAYS OF BUILDING THIS SENSE OF PERSONAL EFFECTIVENESS ARE CONSIDERED—PARTICIPATIVE DECISION MAKING AND ATTRIBUTION MANAGEMENT.

3. THERE ARE BOTH BENEFITS AND COSTS TO A PARTICIPATIVE STYLE OF MANAGEMENT.

4. EFFECTIVE PARTICIPATION REQUIRES CONSIDERATION OF THE TYPES OF DECISIONS BEST SUITED TO THIS APPROACH AND ORGANISATIONAL AND INDIVIDUAL PREREQUISITES.

5. THERE ARE MANY WAYS OF INVOLVING STAFF AND VARIOUS LEVELS OF PARTICIPATION IN DECISION MAKING.

6. A JOINT PROBLEM SOLVING APPROACH IS ONE WAY OF GETTING STAFF INVOLVED.

7. COMMON BLOCKS TO SUCCESSFUL INVOLVEMENT INCLUDE LACK OF A SHARED MISSION, SKILL DEFICITS, LACK OF TIME, CONFLICTS AND RESISTANCE TO CHANGE.

8. ATTRIBUTION DIFFICULTIES INCLUDE FAILING TO PERCEIVE POSITIVE CHANGES, FAILING TO LINK POSITIVE OUTCOMES TO STAFF EFFORT, LINKING NEGATIVE EVENTS TO STAFF ACTIVITY, ASCRIBING NEGATIVE CHARACTERISTICS TO SERVICE USERS.

9. FACTORS THAT CREATE ERRORS OR INACCURACIES IN INTERPRETATIONS INCLUDE POOR QUALITY OF AVAILABLE INFORMATION, PERSONAL BELIEFS OF STAFF, STAFF EMOTIONAL DIFFICULTIES AND THE PROBLEM ORIENTATION OF MOST SERVICES.

10. TECHNIQUES FOR DEALING WITH ATTRIBUTION DIFFICULTIES INCLUDE FOCUSSING ON STRENGTHS, IMPROVING THE QUALITY, BALANCE AND ACCESSIBILITY OF INFORMATION, REINFORCING HELPFUL ATTRIBUTIONS AND CHALLENGING UNHELPFUL ONES, RESOLVING STAFF'S EMOTIONAL DIFFICULTIES.

Manager's toolkit	
Task structuring	Get decisions/problems in to manageable form
Guiding problem solving	Endure participation and quality decisions
Managing meetings	Ensure participation and decision making
Conflict management	Resolve problems, remove blocks
Listening	Increase active participation, decrease emotional difficulties
Reflecting	Decrease emotional difficulties
Questioning	Increase active participation, alter attributions
Summarising	Facilitate decision making, reinforce attributions
Delegating	Increase participation, reinforce attribution
Giving feedback	Reinforce attribution
Devising 'experiments'	Reinforce attribution

CHAPTER 5   What am I here for?

AIMS OF THE CHAPTER

1. TO EXPLAIN THE IMPORTANCE OF CLEAR GOALS TO STAFF MOTIVATION AND PERFORMANCE.

2. TO DEFINE THE CHARACTERISTICS OF EFFECTIVE GOALS.

3. TO DESCRIBE THE DIFFERENT TYPES AND LEVELS OF GOALS.

4. TO IDENTIFY SYSTEMS THAT REFLECT AND SUPPORT AN ACHIEVEMENT ORIENTED CULTURE AT WORK.

INTRODUCTION

Achievement is a very important source of human motivation and activity. Many people are challenged by having problems to solve, goals to aim for. It stimulates them to act and directs their efforts.

Thus having objectives at work will

➤ Motivate many staff
➤ Enable them to organise their work activity in a coherent way

This chapter will look at how to make effective use of such goal setting in the workplace. However, it will go beyond addressing the issue of specific goals for individuals and groups. It will identify a range of work systems which, together, go towards creating a more comprehensive achievement oriented culture. Such a culture will

➤ Stimulate achievement motivation in those to whom it has not been relevant before
➤ Support the achievement motivations in those to whom it is already relevant

A goal oriented culture provides a setting condition in which specific goals can achieve greater effect in terms of strengthening motivation and triggering action.

WHAT CONSTITUTES AN EFFECTIVE GOAL?

In order to be effective in terms of motivating staff and directing their activity a goal needs to meet five criteria (summarised in Table 5.1).

Table 5.1   Criteria for judging effective goals

Goals must be

1. Clear
2. Significant
3. Attainable
4. Reviewed
5. Allocated

1. *Clear*

Goals need to be stated in terms of actual behaviour that can be observed. It sounds wonderful to set staff to

'adopt a positive attitude'
'show commitment'
'help service users to fulfil their potential'
'enhance the quality of life for service users'

Such warm generalities have their place (perhaps!). However, they do not indicate to staff

➤   What they are supposed to do (what counts as 'commitment' or 'quality of life', for example)
➤   How they or anyone else would know when the goal was achieved

Of course what staff do when faced with such 'goals' is either to nod in agreement and then carry on with what they were going to do anyway; or interpret what is said in a more concrete way. The latter is of course very sensible. The difficulty arises if their definition differs from that of their colleagues or manager. Some might interpret quality of life in terms of

keeping users clean, warm and well cared for physically

This may be very different from the manager's intention

to help users experience a wider range of choices in their lives

and

to use community facilities for education, shopping and leisure

Unclear goals run the risk of

➤   Being ineffective
➤   Breeding conflict

An effective goal will be clear and concrete, referring to actual behaviour that can be observed. It will state, at the least

who will do what

and sometimes

with what frequency/to what level of success

Table 5.2   Clear and unclear goals

Unclear
Frank will be less disruptive

Clear
Frank will exhibit no more than two instances of physical aggression to staff or fellow service users in any one day

Unclear
Shahid will become more independent

Clear
Each day Shahid will go on his own to the local newsagent and get a paper or magazine of his choice

Unclear
Mary will take on a key worker role with Siobahn

Clear
Mary will read all background information on Siobahn, will spend at least an hour a week individually with Siobahn, will organise the annual individual programme plan (IPP) review including setting the date, sending out the invitations, preparing a report and chairing the meeting

Unclear
Residents will experience a better quality leisure life

Clear
By the end of next month all residents will have been given the opportunity to attend the local swimming pool, cinema, bingo hall, snooker club, library and shopping precinct

Table 5.2 gives examples of clear and unclear goals.

2.   *Significant*

To mobilise an individual a clear goal must be meaningful to that individual. Staff must value the goals that are set. People will not be motivated to work towards goals that are perceived as

➤ Irrelevant
➤ Unacceptable

This is a particularly difficult point in human services working with people who require high levels of support. The goals of such services are to meet the needs of clients. However, the meeting of these needs depends upon the actions of staff. The fact that a goal is significant for a client does not automatically make it so for the staff. Often the two will coincide but it cannot be assumed.

Example

A goal to teach a person with learning difficulties a new skill will not be seen as significant if staff believe that the client is incapable of learning or that the chosen skill is irrelevant.

The likelihood of this problem arising can be reduced by

➤ Training on client needs and staff values and attitudes
➤ Feedback emphasising the value of particular areas of work
➤ Involving staff in the setting of goals

The outcome needed is that goals set are seen by staff as valuable and significant.

3. *Attainable*

There is no point in setting goals that are fond wishes but have no hope of being achieved. We gave an example in the previous chapter of a service setting staff to help users access community facilities but providing staffing levels that made this impossible. Whilst goals should be attainable they should not necessarily be easy.

➤ People in general are more motivated by difficult goals
➤ Difficult goals raise performance standards, even though staff might experience them as quite stressful

In practice, given that people are often working towards several goals, a spread of difficulty is probably the ideal:

➤ Some goals easy (thereby guaranteeing success experience and satisfaction)
➤ Some harder (thereby raising performance standards).

4. *Reviewed*

Goal setting achieves maximum effectiveness in the context of performance feedback. Feedback on success, progress and difficulties

➤ Sustains motivation
➤ Directs performance

Goals that are set but not monitored or reviewed have a more limited impact upon staff functioning.

5. *Allocated*

A goal is only effective in so far as it is clear who is responsible for its attainment. This is implicit in all the points made above but perhaps needs to be stated explicitly. A goal may be the responsibility of

➤ One person
➤ A small group
➤ A staff team
➤ A whole service

It has to be clear at the time the goal is set who is accountable for the goal being achieved.

WHAT SORTS OF GOALS ARE RELEVANT IN HUMAN SERVICE WORK?

Goals are an 'outcome'—they represent the results to be achieved by staff as a result of 'doing the job'. A number of important outcome areas are likely to be incorporated in goal setting activities. These include

User Attainment

These goals will be set in terms of some change in or maintenance of user behaviour that will result from staff activity.

Examples

Skill mastery or maintenance
Being able to feed oneself, budget money, assert oneself

Behavioural functioning linked to emotional well being
Smiling more, crying less, having fewer panic attacks, sleeping better

Decreases in disadvantaging behaviours
Hitting people less often, breaking fewer items of communal property, smearing faeces less frequently

Much human service work will be reflected in observable user functioning and many of the goals set will reflect this.

User Experience

Human services are not just about what people can do for themselves and how they behave. They are about the experiences that they have, whether or not these are reflected in their immediate behaviour and emotions. Thus some goals will set the staff to effect experiences for service users.

Examples

Use local facilities for shopping and leisure.

Experience a holiday abroad.

Have a friend.

Staff might also be set goals to effect access for users to services that might in turn be expected to impact more directly upon their functioning.

Examples

Attend local education classes.

Access a therapeutic service such as physiotherapy, speech therapy, counselling.

Staff Attainment

How users function and the experiences that they have is dependent upon skilled work by staff. Thus some goals must focus upon staff functioning, maintaining their behaviours and developing new ones.

Examples

Specific job skills
Task analysis of skills for teaching, establishing a behaviour monitoring system

More complex skill clusters (taking on new roles)
Becoming a key worker, becoming a chair person

A good quality working environment will also be seeking to motivate staff by offering personal development programmes (see Chapters 6 and 9), so that some of the goals for staff will reflect this process.

Staff Experience

As with users some goals may be set in terms of staff going through an experience, without direct reference to any effect of the experience on actual behaviour.

Examples

Visit other services.

Meet with other disciplines (for example to discuss roles).

Attend courses or conferences.

Thus the content of goals will focus on the behaviour and experiences of user and staff.

But whatever the content, the goals should be set and expressed in line with the criteria described in the previous section.

OTHER CHARACTERISTICS OF EFFECTIVE GOAL SETTING

Time Span

A crude distinction can be made between short term and long term goals.

A short term goal is one that is targeted for attainment in the immediate future—in our own work we use up to 6–12 weeks as a rough definition of 'immediate'. For 'longer term' our rough definition would be in the region of 6–12 months. How long it takes to achieve a goal will depend upon

➤ The nature of the goal
➤ Characteristics of the individual (staff or user)
➤ Resources available

However, no goal should be set without a date projected for its attainment.

Number of goals

Much service activity will not be driven by a specific goal setting. There will be many activities that are part and parcel of what a service does anyway, on a day to day basis. Goals are used to

➤ Flag up priorities
➤ Focus energy on to key attainments

But there is always a limit to the resources available and this includes a limit as to how much information any one individual can handle.

A staff member faced with having to remember five goals to be worked on each day with five clients has 25 goals to remember and to organise activity towards (?information overload).

As a rough rule

a staff member should not have to be handling more than five to nine items of information at any one time

This argues for great care in the number of goals set, particularly in the most common situation where staff are working with a number of users. When the focus is on one service user, then it is easy to set a large number of goals. But as this becomes multiplied up across a group of service users

➤ The volume of information becomes unmanageable
➤ Staff start to feel overwhelmed
➤ Staff become demotivated

This cancels out all the positive motivational effects of goal setting.

Thus thought needs to be directed towards information management—limiting the number of goals and devising means for enabling these to be classified, recalled and monitored with ease.

GOAL ORIENTED WORK SYSTEMS AND THE CULTURE OF ACHIEVEMENT

In order to set and monitor goals certain systems of work are required. These will enable 'capture' of the achievement motivations that some staff will bring to the workplace.

However, the presence and effective operation of such systems also serve to generate motivation in those who do not already have it.

> **We have been continually impressed by the fact that giving staff clear goals with personal accountability and clear, specific and positively oriented feedback can generate or rekindle enthusiasm in even the most unlikely candidates!**

There are a number of work systems that are required. Their precise method of implementation will vary from workplace to workplace (there are usually many ways of implementing such systems). What is vital is that

> whatever system is used it should actually function on a regular basis

It is no good having systems that function just when

> ➤ A few enthusiasts are around
> ➤ Somebody happens to remember to implement them
> ➤ A crisis arises

A 'flavour of the month' approach will do little other than breed a culture of cynicism.

However, with a range of routine, functioning systems, the whole comes to represent more than the sum of the parts. It creates that setting condition that we have labelled the culture of achievement.

The component systems include

Service Mission–Service Review System

This was also discussed in Chapter 3. A service mission–service review system

> ➤ Sets and reviews goals at the service level
> ➤ Provides the rationale for everyday service activity

Such a system may involve

> ➤ External agencies (service evaluators/inspectors/purchasers)
> ➤ Fellow providers (peer review)
> ➤ Management only
> ➤ Some more participative self review process

There may be more than one approach. There is little evidence as to what constitutes the 'best way', although there is general merit in some independent contribution to the review process.

From the motivational point of view, two characteristics are important:

> ➤ The process should occur regularly
> ➤ There should be active engagement of staff in the review process, whoever is managing it

These characteristics make the system more psychologically effective.

Realistic Job Descriptions

A job description serves as an important reference point at recruitment and at staff monitoring and review. A description that

> states clearly what is expected
> emphasises the sorts of goals towards which a service is aspiring

reinforces the notion of a service and a job that knows where it is going.

Individual Planning Systems—Users

Work systems are needed to

> set

and

> monitor

both long and short term goals for service users. Such systems go under various names— individual programme planning, shared action planning, joint action planning. The name is irrelevant, the function and operation critical.

Individual Planning Systems—Staff

Attention to staff work that is not directly involving users or that targets the development of staff's skills with users, requires a separate work system. Such functions will often form part of appraisal and supervision systems.

Routine Manager–Staff Contact in Real Work Situations (MBWA, Management by Wandering About!)

This is not a formal system like the others mentioned above but a way of day to day working. It emphasises the importance of

> ➤ Contact between management and staff in the course of actual work with service users
> ➤ Feedback about the quality of such work

As well as its technical benefits its regular occurrence makes it clear that quality is about the moment to moment contact between users and providers and the practical, concrete activities that this involves.

An organisation that has functioning and competently implemented systems of work of the kind outlined above will generate as well as support motivation in staff. It will give the message that

> this is a service that knows what it is trying to achieve and knows whether or not it is achieving it

It will be a culture of

>   clear thinking

and

>   straight talking

rather than a culture of fine words and no action.

CONCLUSIONS

Many staff who provide the services that are the focus of this book lack formal qualifications. They may have found formal education a difficult experience and lack the confidence to see themselves as successful and achieving. A framework of supports as discussed above will give them back that confidence and enable them to raise their expectations for themselves and thereby for the service users.

SUMMARY

1. GOALS HELP TO MOTIVATE INDIVIDUALS AND TO DIRECT THEIR ACTIVITIES IN AN EFFECTIVE WAY.

2. A CULTURE OF ACHIEVEMENT CAN GENERATE MOTIVATION IN THOSE NOT ALREADY MOTIVATED IN THIS DIRECTION.

3. IN ORDER TO BE EFFECTIVE GOALS MUST BE CLEAR, SIGNIFICANT, ATTAINABLE, REVIEWED AND ALLOCATED.

4. THE CONTENT ELEMENT OF GOALS WILL FOCUS UPON ATTAINMENT AND EXPERIENCE FOR BOTH USERS AND STAFF ALIKE.

5. GOALS SHOULD BE SET FOR BOTH SHORT (UP TO THREE MONTHS) AND LONG (UP TO 12 MONTHS) TERMS.

6. NO GOAL SHOULD BE SET WITHOUT A DATE PROJECTED FOR ITS ATTAINMENT.

7. THE NUMBER OF GOALS PRIORITISED FOR ANY ONE MEMBER OF STAFF NEEDS TO BE KEPT WITHIN MANAGEABLE BOUNDS.

8. GOAL ORIENTED WORK SYSTEMS INCLUDE SERVICE MISSION AND REVIEW, CLEAR JOB DESCRIPTIONS, INDIVIDUAL PLANNING SYSTEMS FOR BOTH USERS AND STAFF, MANAGEMENT BY WANDERING ABOUT.

9. THE COMBINED EFFECT OF FUNCTIONING GOAL ORIENTED WORK SYSTEMS AT EVERY LEVEL CREATES A CULTURE OF ACHIEVEMENT THAT BOTH GENERATES AND SUPPORTS MOTIVATION.

Manager's toolkit	
Tools	Applications
Goal setting	Support/encourage achievement motivation
Monitoring	Prevent information overload
Give feedback	Indicate significance of goal orientation
Service review	Generate/support achievement motivation
Job description	Generate/support achievement motivation
Individual planning system (users)	Generate/support achievement motivation
Appraisal	Generate/support achievement motivation
Supervision	Generate/support achievement motivation

CHAPTER 6   It's a place to learn

AIMS OF THE CHAPTER

1. TO CONSIDER THE IMPORTANCE OF LEARNING IN PERSONAL
   AND PROFESSIONAL DEVELOPMENT.

2. TO LOOK AT THE PROCESS OF LEARNING.

3. TO CONSIDER HOW LEARNING OPPORTUNITIES CAN BE CRE-
   ATED AND UTILISED WITHIN WORK SETTINGS.

4. TO LOOK AT THE ORGANISATIONAL STRUCTURES WHICH SUP-
   PORT A LEARNING WORK ENVIRONMENT.

INTRODUCTION

The previous chapter looked at ways of building and sustaining achievement motivations in the workplace. The present chapter builds on this, focusing on the role of learning experiences for staff as a contributor to both

> motivation

and

> actual work functioning

Learning is a broad concept. It relates to

➤ Knowledge (knowing about . . .)
➤ Skills (knowing how . . .)
➤ Values (knowing why . . .)

Learning is at the heart of human development (or in the head, if modern theories are to be believed!). All new learning, whether it relates to work, leisure or interpersonal relationships, contributes to an individual's broader personal development.

There has been a tendency to think of development as something confined to the early years of life, as ceasing when full physical maturity is attained. This line of reasoning suggests that by the time a person starts work personal development is completed and it is just a matter now of learning specific job skills. This is a dangerously misguided view! (Q. What are the ages of the authors of this book?!)

> **Development does not end with the attainment of physical maturity**
>
> **is a lifelong process, extending from birth through childhood and adolescence, through early adulthood and the middle years, through retirement to old age**

As

experience of life increases
the circumstances of life evolve

so

skills and knowledge develop
attitudes and values change

As

the individual moves through the developmental cycle

so

personal goals and interests change

Thus at different stages in the cycle and in differing life circumstances an individual will seek to

develop different skills
set different priorities
attain different goals

and will be motivated by different outcomes (or RESULTS in our terminology).

Example

At 18 Debbie started work as an untrained care assistant in a residential establishment for people with learning difficulties. She was keen to learn as much as possible about basic caring.

After a year she was made key worker for one of the residents, a job to which she had aspired for several months. It faced her with a whole new set of challenges—she had to carry out developmental assessments on her key client, write reports, present information at multi-disciplinary meetings, set up monitoring systems to record the client's behaviour, liaise with the day centre and with the client's family.

She became interested in the specific medical condition from which her client was suffering and also in the challenge of helping the client overcome severe behavioural and emotional distur-bances. She wanted further training in these specific areas.

Two years later she was promoted to deputy team leader. She was now faced with new challenges—supervising three junior staff members, taking responsibility for running a shift in the absence of the team leader. The new challenges required new skills—management skills, super-vision skills.

During this time Debbie developed a new interest—that of providing individual counselling to the staff that she was supervising and who were coming to her with personal and work related problems. At the same time her interest in alternative therapies for people with learning difficulties started to grow. Her enjoyment of basic care work was now diminishing.

She spent some time providing individual sessions to clients with specific problems and at the same time taught others about the therapeutic approaches that she used. She became more skilled at this teaching work and her interest in the whole area of staff training grew. She eventually left the organisation for which she was working because there was no scope for her to develop in this direction. She found a job as an assistant training officer with a larger organisation.

Debbie's story is not unusual and reflects how needs and interests change with time and experience.

These needs and interests develop and progress throughout the life cycle. When the workplace does not provide experiences and opportunities relevant to the fulfilment of personal life goals the individual may become frustrated and disgruntled. This leads to outcomes such as

➤ Seeking other employment which offers the relevant opportunities
➤ Apathy and underfunctioning in the present work

Learning and personal development are therefore important sources of satisfaction, important motivators for coming to work. Their absence are important sources of dissatisfaction. Unless the workplace offers opportunities for learning and personal development good calibre staff will prove difficult to retain.

AN EDUCATIONAL WORK CLIMATE?

We will refer to the concept of an educational work climate—making work a place where

➤ Learning and development are valued . . . in general
➤ Learning and development are actively encouraged . . . in planned and specific ways

An educational work climate enables staff to

➤ Improve their existing skills
➤ Make creative use of existing skills to develop new ideas and work related practices
➤ Acquire new knowledge and learn new skills relevant to the present job
➤ Develop skills and knowledge related to longer term personal and career goals
➤ Learn about their own attitudes, values and needs and the influence that these have upon their work behaviour

An educational work climate improves

➤ Job satisfaction
➤ Job performance

It

➤ Influences the desire to come to work (setting condition)
➤ Enhances skill level, actual behaviour at work (action)

➤ Enhances the satisfaction experienced from work (result)
➤ Satisfies specific individual development needs (result)

An educational work climate is therefore a vital contributor to the quality of service actually experienced by users.

DEVELOPING AN EDUCATIONAL WORK CLIMATE

Creating an educational climate in the work environment requires

➤ An understanding of learning processes and media
➤ An understanding of the various opportunities that exist within the work environment for learning and personal development to take place
➤ The use of work systems that support the learning and developmental process, that provide a forum for planning and reviewing relevant learning and developmental experiences for individuals

The Nature of Learning

Learning encompasses three main areas.

1. The Acquisition of Knowledge

Knowledge gives a broader understanding of specific phenomena that people have to deal with at work. Examples include knowing about

➤ The theoretical foundations for a particular approach to understanding behaviour
➤ Group processes and dynamics
➤ Specific conditions such as autism
➤ Specific biological processes such as Alzheimer's disease
➤ The favourite foods and hobbies of an individual client
➤ The cultural background of individual service users

2. The Acquisition of Skills

> Knowledge . . . in principle
> . . . is not the same as
> skill . . . in practice

Knowing in principle how to drive a car is no guarantee of competence the first time that a person gets behind the wheel! Understanding the principles of a particular therapeutic approach does not mean that one is able to apply that approach in a skilled way with a particular client. Thus the acquisition of skills needs consideration in its own right as an area of learning.

3.   The Acquisition of Values

Values are deeply held beliefs (not always conscious) that influence one's personal priorities and the standards and interpretations that one applies to the situations that occur in life.

Examples

A person who believes that people with learning disabilities have the mentality of children will think about and behave towards those individuals as she does to other children. A person who believes that all human life should be respected and all human beings valued, whatever their disability, will interact in a respectful way with individuals in the late stages of senile dementia, despite the fact that the client may not understand or recognise the person.

Good quality human service work requires an underpinning of certain key values. Staff will not necessarily come 'ready made' with these values. The acquisition of these values is therefore an important focus of development.

Supporting people with long term disabilities and complex physical and psychological needs, usually in a team work context, requires a range of

➤   Knowledge
➤   Skills
➤   Values

The competences may relate to

➤   The particular client group
➤   Working effectively within a team
➤   Forming constructive personal relationships with others
➤   Organising oneself and the work process

In such work the potential for personal development and learning is extensive. However, realising this potential requires an understanding of the various ways in which learning occurs.

How Learning Takes Place

1.   Knowledge

Knowledge is based upon the symbolic representation of particular experiences. It is about acquiring a more general understanding of specific encounters. Acquisition occurs by a range of methods.

➤   Listening (talks, lectures, seminars)
➤   Reading (books, articles)
➤   Observing (real life, videos)

➤ Reflecting (upon personal experience, the witness accounts of others)
➤ Remembering (making links between specific experiences)

2. Skills

Skills are acquired by

➤ Observation
➤ Direct practice
➤ Feedback on performance

Learning through observation. Observing other people perform a task . . . and succeed at that task . . . can be an effective way to learn because

➤ Having observed another succeed gives encouragement to perform the task in the same manner
➤ A 'live' demonstration of how to perform an activity is less ambiguous than being told about it or reading about it. The more frequently the performance of the task is observed, the more details can be taken in

Learning by observation may occur formally or incidentally.

Example

New staff will observe more experienced staff handling difficult situations or clients and will emulate their approach if it is seen to be effective.

Key fact: people are more likely to learn from models whom they respect or identify with.

Thus during everyday work a respected manager or senior staff member will be watched and copied by newer or less experienced staff. This makes it vital that managers/ supervisors

➤ Model good practices
➤ Avoid modelling bad practices (for example, arriving late, shouting at service users)
➤ Be available frequently to model

Learning through direct practice. Modelling indicates what to do and gives the encouragement to do it. Mastery of skills, however, develops through direct practice. Practice can occur in a number of ways, some of which are more productive than others, depending upon the situation.

Experimentation and discovery: this is appropriate when there is no best way to perform a task, no specific solution to be achieved.

Example

Finding out what types of activities a person enjoys can be done by asking, observing, showing pictures or videos, getting the individual to have a go . . . with no one method being necessarily better than any other.

Trial and error: this occurs when it is clear *what* needs to be achieved . . . but it is not clear *how* it is to be achieved. Things are tried, mistakes occur but in the end a solution is found.

Example

A client has severe behavioural outbursts and the reasons are not clear. It is important to help the person avoid such outbursts and to manage them safely if they do occur. A number of methods are tried systematically until the best method is found.

Trial and error learning may be necessary if the solution is not known or if there is no-one available to help. However, such learning can take a long time, may be discouraging and can expose users to unnecessary risks.

Structured learning: if it is clear what is to be achieved and if someone knows how the task is to be performed then learning can be enhanced by specific forms of help and encouragement:

➤   Written/verbal/pictorial instructions
➤   Demonstration
➤   General pointers
➤   Breaking the task down and learning it bit by bit
➤   Giving praise and encouragement for correct performance
➤   Giving additional help when errors are made

The person managing the learning process therefore organises this in a structured way, using the above techniques so that it is very likely that the learning occurs successfully and with the minimum of errors.

Example

There is only one safe way to deal with a particular individual when she becomes distressed or agitated. A new staff member is

−   told what the method is
−   shown how to do it when the person next becomes agitated
−   given the chance to practise the method with the 'teacher' observing
−   given extra help by the 'teacher' if things go wrong
−   praised if the situation is handled successfully

Learning through feedback on performance. Detailed feedback on performance leads to more effective learning than praise on its own. Such feedback requires that the 'teacher'

> Separate out the components of the task
> Detail the components that were carried out successfully
> Explain why they were correct
> Detail the components that were carried out unsuccessfully
> Explain why they were incorrect

Example

The new member of staff is observed calming the client who has become agitated and is told how well he handled the situation:
'You spoke to her in a calm and confident voice
You approached her quietly and calmly
But
When you tried to distract her you offered too many choices and she became confused, with the result that her agitation increased.'

Clear, concrete feedback with an accompanying explanation is a very powerful way of shaping up staff performance.

3.   Values

Values are deeply held beliefs. They are the product of a lifetime's learning and experience, influenced by parents, teachers, friends, other respected role models and by society in general. Thus changing values means more than handing a staff member a written mission statement on her first day at work. It means getting staff members to believe in the values, not just telling them about the values that underpin a service.

Such beliefs can be developed by

> Education–training programmes which encourage exploration of values and provide reasons for the values underpinning the service
> Observation of practice which exemplifies the values in action
> Respect for other individuals who hold such values
> Group dynamics—wishing to be accepted by groups who hold these values
> Encouragement of specific performances which exemplify the values in action— behaviour change tends to drive attitude change, not the other way around

Creating and Making Full Use of Learning Opportunities

The workplace is potentially rich in learning opportunities for staff. In addition to those naturally occurring opportunities managers can create more formal learning opportunities by

> Making available up-to-date reading materials relevant to the job (books, journals, articles) and ensuring that information about new developments and new knowledge is provided for staff

➤ Using regular staff meetings to practise and improve team work skills, making good use of performance feedback

➤ Observing staff carrying out routine tasks and providing positive and constructive feedback on their performance

➤ Providing direct instruction and coaching with feedback for important skills such as report writing, handling aggressive clients, devising IPPs

➤ Delegating to staff tasks that provide new developmental challenges and that allow individuals to develop specialist skills, knowledge and interests

➤ Setting up, and encouraging staff to set up, innovative projects to improve the quality of service being provided

➤ Organising in-house training for staff teams

➤ Arranging visits to other establishments or job exchange schemes in order to observe the working practices of other services

➤ Sending staff on external training courses in order to acquire specific knowledge and skills

As with other areas covered in this book

it is not that there is one right way to stimulate learning and develop an educational climate

but rather

that there are many ways to achieve these goals

. . . and this allows for flexibility and adjustment to the individual circumstances of a service.

Structures which Support a Learning Environment

In order to maximise the number and relevance of learning opportunities available to staff three formal work systems/structures are helpful.

1. Staff Appraisal and Career Development Counselling

Appraisal systems have a number of functions in relation to improving the effectiveness of an organisation. Appraisal systems can

➤ Identify the individual developmental needs/aspirations of staff

➤ Set longer term targets around those identified needs (to enhance performance in the present job and to develop new skills for positive career moves in the future)

➤ Monitor staff performance overall

➤ Generate information on the kinds of training that staff need in order to function effectively . . . and thereby deliver a quality service

2. Staff Supervision

Supervision, like appraisal, has many functions. It can effect change in staff by

Imparting new knowledge. Passing relevant information, explaining reasons for current practices including theoretical perspectives.

Reinforcing good practice. Giving clear feedback on things done well.

Correcting poor practice. Giving clear feedback on things not done well.

Learning from experience. Reviewing specific incidents to see what can be learned in relation to future action.

Planning staff learning/development. Working out the details of how and when identified knowledge/skills are to be acquired and monitoring progress on this.

Exploration of values and attitudes. Relating everyday work to underlying values, drawing out the beliefs and attitudes of the staff member, challenging those beliefs and attitudes which are at variance with service requirements.

3.   A Training Policy

If an organisation is committed to

> enhancing the job skills of staff
> developing the talents of employees
> facilitating internal promotion and advancement
> helping staff to meet career and personal development needs

then coherent policies will be required in order to ensure that needs are identified and resources directed in a rational way.

A commitment to training, and the policy that grows out of this, will

➤   Help the organisation enhance staff performance
➤   Increase the job satisfaction of staff
➤   Enable the organisation to develop its own human resources and facilitate internal promotion

A training policy will need to address a number of areas:

The immediate job to be done. The skills required to function effectively. This is likely to form part of an induction programme for new staff.

The work environment. Knowing about the organisation and the particular client group. This may be incorporated as part of the induction programme or be dealt with in supervision.

Promotion and advancement. Learning relevant to a more senior job (for example, supervisory skills, staff motivation, quality control).

Specialisation. Learning which enables development within current job functioning (for example, learning about behaviour analysis, bereavement counselling, reminiscence therapy).

Efficiency enhancement. Learning for working more efficiently (for example, team skills, information technology skills).

Appraisal and supervision systems and formal training policies provide the structures whereby developmental targets can be

> set, in collaboration with staff

and

> followed through on

Within these structures

➤ Progress can be reviewed
➤ Difficulties and problems can be pinpointed
➤ Solutions can be explored

However, these structures alone will not be sufficient to develop and sustain an 'educational work climate'. Learning opportunities, formal and informal, need to be made available to staff so that they can work towards their individual developmental goals, whilst continuing to fulfil the immediate requirements of their jobs.

SUMMARY

1. LEARNING IS THE ACQUISITION OF KNOWLEDGE, SKILLS AND VALUES. EACH CAN BE LEARNED THROUGH A VARIETY OF MEDIA.

2. LEARNING AND DEVELOPMENT IS A LIFELONG PROCESS.

3. THE DEVELOPMENT OF WORK AND PERSONAL SKILLS IS A MAJOR SOURCE OF MOTIVATION AND SATISFACTION AT WORK.

4. THE SKILLS AND KNOWLEDGE LEARNED IN ANY JOB ARE OFTEN SEEN BY INDIVIDUALS AS STEPPING STONES TO JOB ADVANCEMENT AND PROMOTION.

5. AN ORGANISATIONAL COMMITMENT TO HELPING INDIVIDUAL EMPLOYEES DEVELOP SKILLS AND FULFIL THEIR CAREER AND PERSONAL GOALS WILL ENHANCE GENERAL MOTIVATION TO COME TO WORK AND WILL IMPROVE JOB PERFORMANCE.

6. ADVANTAGE NEEDS TO BE TAKEN OF THE MANY LEARNING OPPORTUNITIES AVAILABLE WITHIN THE WORKPLACE TO FACILITATE THE DEVELOPMENT OF STAFF.

7. APPRAISAL AND SUPERVISION SYSTEMS ARE ORGANISA-
TIONAL STRUCTURES WHICH ASSIST THE DELIVERY OF A STAFF
DEVELOPMENT POLICY.

8. A COMPREHENSIVE STAFF TRAINING POLICY IS REQUIRED IF
AN EDUCATIONAL WORK CLIMATE IS TO BE SUSTAINED.

Manager's toolkit	
Tools	Applications
Modelling	Demonstrating and encouraging use of specific job skills Demonstrating values in action and encouraging adoption of values
Didactic teaching	Imparting knowledge
Questioning	Imparting knowledge. Effecting change in values
Task analysis	Making a work task accessible to staff
Praising	Encouraging staff in specific actions
Giving feedback	Giving information about required staff actions. Encouraging/discouraging specific staff actions
Developing teamwork	Producing social pressure to adopt values
Goal setting	Improving specific staff performances
Delegation	Developing achievement motivation. Encouraging ownership of ideas/practices
Appraisal	Identifying and monitoring staff development needs
Supervision	Supporting good practice. Effecting change in staff functioning
Policy writing	Develop coherent approach to staff development
Being organised	Make learning opportunities available to staff

CHAPTER 7   Good people to work with?

INTRODUCTION

Much of this book considers the ways in which a manager can influence the motivation and behaviour of staff . . . on an individual level. However, a quality service to people with long term disabilities requires not just that staff function well

 on an individual basis

but that they work together . . .

 as a team

Helping people with extensive, long term disabilities requires work day in, day out. Development–therapy–education . . . whatever term is used . . . does not occur in special places where somebody (client–patient–student) goes temporarily, for short periods of time.

It is part and parcel of everyday interactions between provider and user.

Given that paid providers work limited hours this means that providers need to work together in a coordinated way if users are to get maximum benefit from the services provided. Indeed in many professional care settings it requires the coordinated effort of three or four groups of people, working in shifts to cover 24 hours a day, seven days a week.

Thus teamwork is essential to the quality of service provision for people with long term difficulties. A team approach operates in a number of ways to achieve this outcome.

THE EFFECTS THAT GROUP RELATIONSHIPS HAVE

Creating Setting Conditions

Many people are motivated to belong to and identify with groups. Cohesive groups offer the opportunity to satisfy a wide range of social motivations. These include the opportunity to experience

➤ Having a useful role
➤ Belonging
➤ Being valued
➤ Being liked
➤ Being with people who share a similar interest

A good functioning group will also

➤ Offer support to individuals in difficulty
➤ Buffer against stress
➤ Reduce the impact of stress induced motivations

Conversely a non-cohesive group will fail to generate and support positive motivations and fail to buffer against stress. If active conflict is also present in the group then a wide range of alternative motivations will be generated—motivations around

➤ Anger
➤ Anxiety
➤ Confusion
➤ Sadness

These will tend to generate fight, flight or freeze behaviours in relation to fellow group members and this can only be detrimental to those who use the service.

Creating Triggers

A good functioning team will set clear standards for each member of the group and in many informal ways prompt compliance with these standards. Likewise mutual help will occur readily. As long as the group sees itself as there to deliver a quality service to users such group processes will be a positive force. Conversely if the group

is not cohesive
is in active conflict
does not see its purpose as user led

then quality will be diminished.

Creating Actions

Team efforts and team problem solving can be far superior to the efforts and solutions of individuals working in isolation. Thus a positive team approach will affect the actual work carried out with users, the everyday behaviour of staff. Conversely . . .

Creating Results

Group processes will shape the actions of individual team members by giving or withholding results for behaviours, results such as

➤ Praise
➤ Approval
➤ Respect
➤ Liking
➤ Valuing

A well functioning group concerned with service quality will thus have built in, formally and informally, a network of contingencies supportive of good practice. The converse again is obvious.

Thus the social environment and the group processes within it are a vital focus for a manager. The aim is to

➤ Create and maintain a positive work climate
➤ Harness the combined energy and talents of the individuals within the group

In this way STAFF and USERS are more likely to

➤ Attain to the best of their capability
➤ Experience satisfaction

BUILDING TEAMWORK—BASIC REQUIREMENTS

Teams do not just happen. They have to be built . . . and once built they have to be looked after . . . otherwise there is a risk of

➤ Disintegration
➤ Loss of effectiveness
➤ Reversion to a group of individuals working within the same place

Teams are inherently unstable . . . they need regular attention.

There are a number of basic conditions that need to be met if a group of people is to function as a team. These include

A Common Purpose

There cannot be a team unless all the individuals agree on the 'game' that is to be played. A 'game' involves

➤ Having clear and agreed goals that are to be achieved
➤ Goals that require the coordinated effort of all the players—they cannot be achieved by an individual acting alone
➤ Rules that indicate what is and is not allowed in terms of how things are to be done

this is of course the concept of a mission. A team's mission may be somewhat different from the general mission of an organisation, depending upon the size and diversity of the organisation. It must relate directly to the overall mission but in a way that is geared to the specific client group or needs that the team is working for.

A Team Philosophy

This is a sub-section of the mission which expresses a clear commitment to a team approach and spells that out in terms of specific values and attitudes. These might include such statements as:

Team members will
- respect one another as people and one another's opinions
- value each other's efforts
- acknowledge that the work is difficult and stressful
- acknowledge that successes are achieved by team effort and cooperation

Behavioural Norms

These are a written set of rules that govern the behaviour of each member of the team at work. Each team will have its own set of norms but examples might include rules about

➤ Punctuality
➤ Smoking
➤ Not gossiping about team members
➤ Not criticising people behind their backs
➤ Behaviour toward service users such as forms of address, tone of voice etc.

The participation of team members in the construction of the team mission, the team philosophy and the team behavioural norms constitute a team building exercise in itself.

Understanding of Each Other

For people to work well together they need to understand what they can expect of each other—what other individuals

➤ Can or cannot do
➤ Will or will not do

Each member also has to understand how she is seen and understood by other members of the team.
Without this understanding (sensitivity)

➤ Communication failures will occur
➤ People will be asked to do things that are beyond their reach
➤ People will not be asked to do things that are within their reach

The team will not work well together.

However, in addition to understanding each other as individuals team members will need to understand the various roles that they have in the team. There are the

➤ Formal team roles—such as team leader, team secretary
➤ Individual team member roles—such as key worker, speech therapist
➤ Informal team roles—this is a concept introduced by Belbin (1981) which offers an additional perspective on the makings of a successful team. The ideas are outlined in Table 7.1

Table 7.1   Team roles (from Belbin 1981)

Role title	Main actions
Chair	Clarifies purposes Sees to allocation of responsibilities Summarises decisions Reflects feelings Recalls past successes
Shaper	Draws out themes in discussion Suggests possible decisions Helps detail action/implementation plans
Plant	Makes/challenges/suggestions/ideas
Company worker	Translates ideas into practical action steps
Team worker	Focusses on process issues—supporting and encouraging others, resolving conflicts/disruption
Resource investigator	Brings in ideas from the outside Makes/maintains contacts with other groups/individuals
Monitor/evaluator	Analyses problems/situations/tasks Introduces information Evaluates contributions of others
Completer	Checks the fine details of decisions/action plans Checks others for follow through on agreed tasks

All these roles are important to understand. According to Belbin (1981), who has developed the concept of informal roles, each person has a preferred role or roles within a team. For a team to be effective all the roles need to be filled. The manager needs to ensure that

➤ All roles are filled
➤ Each team member understands her own role
➤ Each team member understands the roles that other team members have

Informal roles need to be acknowledged as well as formal roles and all members need to understand that each role depends upon every other role for its effectiveness.

Honesty and Trust

These terms mean that each member of the group

- Can rely on what every other member says—what people say they do in fact believe, people will try to do what they say they will do
- Knows that fellow team members will celebrate successes and support when things that are tried go wrong
- Can rely on the fact that the information that they reveal about themselves will not be used against them in any way

Without such trust

- Honest, open communication will not be possible
- Mutual understanding will be undermined

Teamwork will be impaired.

Participative Decision Making

Working together to make decisions

- Gives experience of team working in and of itself
- Increases mutual understanding (listening to each other)
- Increases trust (decisions get made and are acted upon)

The concept of participation is central to the building of teamwork and a team approach. However, for this to occur skilled management of the process is required (see Chapter 5). In particular getting the group involved in systematic problem solving is a good way to strengthen cohesion. Using the model outlined earlier the group works together to

- Define a problem
- Identify all possible options for solving it
- Evaluate the various options identified
- Select a favoured option
- Identify action steps to implement the solution
- Allocate responsibilities for tasks to various team members
- Monitor and review progress

Clear Goals

Linked to the notion of joint problem solving, teamwork is developed when goals are set for the staff group as a whole or for sub-groups of staff. This gives very concrete tasks for the group around which it can

work together

and

receive feedback

These are some of the fundamental requirements for building teamwork and a team approach to work tasks. Once the fundamentals are addressed there are a number of more specific techniques for strengthening a team.

BUILDING TEAMWORK—ADDITIONAL APPROACHES

Below are a range of concrete suggestions for enhancing team functioning. The list is not exhaustive and the approaches are supplementary to, not a replacement for, those mentioned in the previous section.

Affirmation of Commitment to the Team and its Collective Purpose

A public statement by individual members about their commitment to

> the team
> its task
> teamwork in general

is a way of keeping alive the team ethos. It reminds people that

➤ They are not working alone and in isolation
➤ Individual goals and efforts must be aligned to those of the rest of the team

Such affirmations can be made, for example, at the start of team meetings.

Identify the Individual Strengths and Talents of Team Members

Team members have formal and informal roles. They also bring to their work a wealth of

➤ Prior experience
➤ Interests
➤ Hobbies
➤ Talents

These are a resource for the team and the exercise of identifying the strengths of each team member

➤ Increases mutual understanding
➤ Suggests ways in which a team might offer a more unique approach

For example, the special interests of staff members (the musician, the sports person, the race goer, the pastry cook, the explorer etc.) can be used to enrich the lives of service users by offering access to new opportunities.

Establish a Team Identity

There are many ways to help a team establish its own independent identity:

A name. The team can give itself a name that represents its task or personality. Communications from the team can then be signed with the team name. This strengthens the sense of group rather than individual action.

A logo. The team can design its own logo or symbol, which represents the team and is included in all team paperwork.

A t-shirt/sweatshirt. With the team name or logo.

Listing team characteristics. The team can write out a list of its identifying characteristics, which distinguish it from other teams. This can be displayed and regularly reviewed/revised.

Listing team achievements. Important achievements can be listed and displayed. Again regular updating is helpful.

Additional Joint Projects

Work with service users

➤   May be difficult
➤   Will usually be long term
➤   Will not always be successful

It may assist the development of team functioning if other kinds of joint projects are established. Examples include

➤   Getting staff to plan a training programme for themselves
➤   Getting staff to plan a social outing for themselves as a group
➤   Using the team building games that can be found in a number of publications

Tough Times Goal Setting

There will be times in human service work when major difficulties arise with service users—for example

➤   Major losses in personal function
➤   Actively disturbed and challenging behaviours

These sorts of problems may prove on occasions very difficult to resolve satisfactorily. This can mean

➤   Morale drops
➤   Teamwork comes apart

In these circumstances it is important to

>   avoid exclusive focus on the most intractable problems facing the team
>   look for additional short term projects (as above)

set some easily achievable goals for the work group

so that

there is experience of success to counter the difficulties and sense of failure

Specific Activities to Enhance Mutual Understanding

There are a number of simple activities that will enhance understanding between group members.

Keeping the circle. It is important to keep to a circle arrangement for all joint discussion and planning meetings. Everyone needs to be able

to see

everybody else

to hear

if good communication and understanding is to be achieved. Drifting to

squares
rows
arrangements where people are left out of/can withdraw from the group

undermines effective communication and mutual understanding.

There are exercises done in pairs which can make a contribution to improved mutual understanding. Over time it is essential that everyone works with everyone else on these exercises if the benefit to the team is to be maximised. These exercises include

Getting to know more about you. Pairs discuss topics that reveal important information about themselves. Examples of topics include

➤ Things that make me happy/sad/angry . . . and how I show my feelings
➤ Best and worst life experiences that I have had
➤ Things I like/dislike about work
➤ Things at which I think I am good/bad

These exercises need to be structured with the topics set and set times for each member of the pair to speak on the topic . . . and for the partner to listen.

Circle checks. This technique, mentioned in Chapter 4, is a way of ensuring that each member of the group makes a statement without further comment or questioning from others—that is

speaks honestly and is listened to by everyone else

Chapter 4 illustrated its use in group problem solving, to get an opinion from each group member on their personally preferred course of action. Circle checks can also be used to

get group members to express how they feel emotionally about a particular topic or situation

The circle check needs to be woven into the process of joint planning and decision making rather than being a separate exercise.

Appreciations. Each member of the group expresses an appreciation about every other member of the group:

> something that they feel positive about and would want the other person to continue doing

This can be said directly to the individual. More often it will involve

first

> writing down the appreciation

then

> saying it to the other in a 1 : 1 situation

As confidence is gained it may be possible to do this as a group—members addressing each other directly in front of the whole team.

Requests. Each member of the group expresses a request to every other member of the group:

> something that they would like the other to do less/more of

This can be said directly to the individual. More often it will involve

first

> writing down the request

then

> saying it to the other in a 1 : 1 situation

As confidence is gained it may be possible to do this as a group—members addressing each other directly in front of the whole team.

The appreciations and requests exercises can be combined into a single exercise.

Appreciations and request exercises can

➤ Be carried out as part of ordinary team activities
➤ Form part of specific team building which is separated from business activities

Regular Process Review

Team functioning may be enhanced if the team regularly sets aside time to reflect on how it is working as opposed to what it is doing. This may

➤ Be put as a separate 'agenda' item at a business meeting
➤ Form a separate occasion

It is often helpful if the discussion is preceded by reflection. Getting team members to

> write down the strengths and needs of the team
> complete rating scales on team functioning

will help to focus the discussion and to remind team members about important process variables to consider.

Enhancing the Salience of Positive Competition

A group's functioning may be enhanced by pressures from outside the group. The most common form of pressure is threat or criticism—something negative will happen if the group does not do better. The trouble with threats is that whilst they can unite a group,

> they can just as easily split it

Even if solidarity is enhanced the group behaviour suggested is likely to be negatively driven—to escape from the threat by

➤   Attacking the source
➤   Complying just until the threat is lifted

These outcomes are not ideal from a quality of human service point of view.
Far better may be to set about a positive struggle for excellence. This will mean

➤   Looking at other services to see how one can do better than them
➤   Using regular service audit information not from a threat point of view but from an opportunity point of view

Locating the service group in terms of positive external pressure can be a very effective way of

➤   Building teamwork
➤   Raising team performance

Bring in an External Team Builder

This book comes from a strong self help orientation. Nevertheless there may be times when use of an external consultant or facilitator will assist team development. Some services will identify someone with a permanent role to look at interpersonal functioning and teamwork.

The 'staff group' run by someone with a 'psychotherapeutic' background is a common model of this approach.

Other services may prefer to use external consultants on a more temporary basis

➤   When a group is stuck
➤   As part of regular service audit/review

There is no indication as to whether one approach is better than another. However, it is important for all staff to recognise that

> teamwork is everybody's responsibility

There is a danger in using 'outsiders' that this responsibility becomes seen as the consultant's.

REVIEWING TEAM FUNCTIONING

Mention has already been made of the need for regular process review. There is also need for a less frequent (?annually) but more comprehensive review of team functioning, as a means of both

> monitoring

and

> strengthening

team development. The focus is not on service users and their problems but on the team itself.

This kind of review requires a clear allocation of time, of the order of a half or a whole day. Such an exercise may benefit from the use of a person outside the team, to facilitate the process. The key questions to address are

➤ How are we doing with regard to our assigned tasks?
➤ How are our relationships with each other?
➤ What problems do we have that we should work on?
➤ What are we doing right?
➤ What are we doing wrong?

Initially, the team may start by addressing these issues in pairs or small groups. Then . . .

➤ Information is pooled
➤ Themes are identified
➤ Issues are discussed
➤ Priority areas of work are agreed
➤ Possible solutions are reviewed
➤ Action steps are decided on
➤ Tasks are allocated and monitoring procedures agreed

The team finishes with an evaluation of its performance during the session.

MANAGING CONFLICTS WITHIN THE TEAM

Conflicts can occur for many reasons—they may be based upon differences in

➤ Attitudes
➤ Values
➤ Motives
➤ Opinions
➤ Feelings

➤ Behavioural style

Conflict is inevitable . . . indeed it is desirable. Teams where no-one disagrees, where everything is accepted, will not develop, will not be creative (the phenomenon of 'groupthink'). Constructive conflict can

➤ Introduce different solutions to a problem
➤ Challenge assumptions—encourage creativity
➤ Highlight individual contributions
➤ Bring into the open emotive arguments
➤ Release tension

However, if conflict is not addressed, if differences remain unresolved, damage will occur both to the individuals in conflict and to the team as a whole. Destructive conflict can

➤ Split the group into factions with polarised views
➤ Stimulate a win–lose approach rather than a search for consensus and negotiated outcomes
➤ Block effective communication
➤ Subvert task oriented activities in favour of relationship oriented activities (tasks become a means of 'settling scores')
➤ Create mistrust and suspicion

If conflict cannot be resolved in a common sense informal way, by getting people to

discuss their differences

and

come to a solution

then a more formal method can be adopted. A useful format for doing this is presented in Table 7.2 (see also Chapter 4). It offers a systematic way of getting each party to

➤ Listen to the other
➤ Communicate with the other
➤ Acknowledge alternative viewpoints
➤ Reach a solution

HELPING RELATED TEAMS TO WORK TOGETHER

A quality overall service often requires the input of more than one team. These teams may be part of a single service (for example, shifts in a residential service). They may be part of different services (for example, day and residential services). Work between teams may be

uncoordinated

and marked by

poor communication
mutual criticism and distrust

Table 7.2   Managing conflict within a team

* Set time aside for this exercise with the whole team present
* Ensure that team members are aware of the purpose of the exercise

1. Identify the conflicting positions and the reasons for those positions

2. Encourage everyone to express their opinion, their thoughts or doubts etc.

3. Divide the team into two subgroups according to the position to which they are closest (an alternative is to mix the groups so that some have to argue against the position that they hold). The groups are assigned the tasks of formally and in turn presenting and defending their positions

4. The other group are instructed to:
   listen as the argument is presented
   ask only questions which ask for more information, clarification of specific points, explanations etc.
   reflect back to the other group the position that has been presented ('As we understand it, this is the view that you take and your reasons for it . . .')

5. After both sides have presented their case and understanding has been checked, reaffirm the common goal of the team

6. Each group identifies the strengths of the opposing argument

7. Possible solutions to the problems are then generated and evaluated

8. A consensus agreement is sought

9. Necessary action steps are agreed

10. The whole process and its outcome is summarised

Example

At St Juliette's, a residential establishment for people with profound learning difficulties the staff are divided into two shift teams. Each shift has its own leader, responsible to the manager. The shifts meet briefly via a 15 minute overlap period. They rarely meet as a complete working team. Over time each shift has developed its own values and norms and its own way of working with service users. This has led to conflicts and resentments. Shift A believes that tasks such as cleaning are secondary to spending quality time with service users. Shift B believes that hygiene and cleanliness is the first and most important task of the team and they devote more time to this than to direct client work. Shift B complains that Shift A always leaves the home in a mess when they finish. Shift A complains that service users engage in very few activities when Shift B is at work.

This is illustrative of a very common cause for intergroup conflict—differences in values, norms and priorities.

Whilst conflict may be uncomfortable for staff the real losers are those who use the service. The service they receive is uncoordinated, inconsistent and confusing. The atmosphere is uncomfortable.

If such situations are recognised then relatively simple steps can be taken to

➤ Reduce conflict
➤ Promote harmony and cohesion

The exact solution to the problem of course depends upon the exact nature of the conflict. Options include

Joint Work on Mission/Philosophy/Objectives (see earlier)

The groups can be helped to understand that they are working towards the same shared goals.

Joint Work on Practical Activities

This might include

➤ Finding a common goal for both groups to work on
➤ Identifying a 'competitor' that both groups can work towards exceeding in terms of service quality
➤ Cross fertilisation activities such as periods of discussion, observation or job exchange with the other group

Formal Inter-team Building Exercises

This is similar to the team review mentioned in the previous section and requires time to be set aside when both teams meet and work together. Again, use of an outside facilitator may be of value. One way of using this time to promote better joint working would be to work through the series of stages outlined in Table 7.3.

Table 7.3   Inter-team building exercise

1. Each team writes down
    – its thoughts, attitudes and feelings about the other group
    – how the other group blocks effective delivery of services to users
    – a list of strengths that it sees in the other group
    – what they think the other team will be writing about them in response to these questions

2. The teams exchange the information from 1

3. The teams work in their own groups to discuss their reactions to what the other group have written—what they have learned about themselves as a team and about the other group

* At this stage many problems which have been perceived as existing between the groups disappear

4. Each group writes a list of priorities which the two groups must work on in order to resolve remaining differences

5. The groups share their information, action steps are agreed, responsibilities allocated and follow-up dates fixed to review progress

6. Each group gives a summary statement as to how it will be behaving differently as a result of the exercise

** The range of the team building activities mentioned earlier in the chapter could also be adapted to promoting better working relationships across two teams

CONCLUSIONS

Effective teamwork has an enormous impact upon the quality of service to people with long term, often hard to understand, difficulties. Team building itself is sometimes elevated to almost mystical status, being seen as immensely complex and requiring bizarre interventions by professional 'team builders'. Whilst the dynamics of relationships within a group can be complex and obscure, they are not necessarily so. There are many practical activities that ordinary mortals can undertake in order to enhance the effectiveness of any working group.

SUMMARY

1. GOOD TEAMWORK MAKES A SIGNIFICANT CONTRIBUTION TO THE QUALITY OF A SERVICE FOR ITS USERS; AND TO STAFF MOTIVATION AND SATISFACTION.

2. BENEFITS OF GOOD TEAMWORK TO USERS INCLUDE MORE CREATIVE PROBLEM SOLVING AND A BETTER ATMOSPHERE AROUND THEM.

3. BENEFITS TO STAFF OF GOOD TEAMWORK INCLUDE THE BENEFITS TO USERS AND GAINING A SENSE OF IDENTITY, FRIENDSHIP AND SUPPORT DURING TIMES OF DIFFICULTY.

4. TEAMWORK CAN ONLY DEVELOP WHEN THERE IS A SHARED SENSE OF PURPOSE, MUTUAL UNDERSTANDING, HONESTY AND TRUST.

5. HAVING A CLEAR MISSION, SPECIFIC GOALS FOR THE WORK GROUP, PARTICIPATIVE DECISION MAKING AND ROUTINE REVIEWS OF SERVICE FUNCTIONING ALL MAKE A CONTRIBUTION TO TEAM DEVELOPMENT.

6. OTHER ACTIVITIES WHICH CAN BE USED TO ENHANCE TEAM FUNCTIONING INCLUDE SHORT TERM GROUP PROJECTS, TEAM BUILDING GAMES, PROCESS REVIEWS AND SPECIFIC EXERCISES TO DEVELOP COMMUNICATION AND MUTUAL UNDERSTANDING BETWEEN TEAM MEMBERS.

7. RELATING THE SERVICE TO OTHER SIMILAR SERVICES IN TERMS OF POSITIVE COMPETITION WILL ALSO ASSIST TEAM DEVELOPMENT.

8. A TEAM NEEDS TO TAKE TIME OUT EVERY SO OFTEN TO REVIEW MORE COMPREHENSIVELY ITS FUNCTIONING.

9. CONFLICTS WITHIN A TEAM REQUIRE ACTIVE MANAGEMENT.

10. CONFLICTS BETWEEN DIFFERENT TEAMS WHICH CONTRIBUTE TO THE OVERALL SERVICE TO USERS REQUIRE ACTIVE MANAGEMENT.

Manager's toolkit	
Tools	Applications
Involve staff in decision making	Increase commitment to decisions
Set group goals/projects	Develop joint working practices by staff
Observation	Identify conflicts between staff members
Mediation	Resolve conflicts
Select/implement communication and team building exercises	Enhance staff group functioning
Give feedback	Influence group/individual behaviour, enhance understanding of self and needs of others
Select/devise job aids	Assist review of team functioning
Identify similar services	Develop positive competition
Identify consultant	Assist team building
Manage meetings	Effect joint problem solving and decision making. Resolve conflicts

CHAPTER 8   The right frame of mind

AIMS OF THE CHAPTER

1. To describe practical ways of making strong and salient the motivations that are central to good quality work in human services.

INTRODUCTION

Previous chapters have outlined ways in which the workplace can be organised and managed so that important motivations are created and supported, motivations to

➤ Be a helper to another
➤ Achieve task success
➤ Enhance personal development
➤ Gain social approval
➤ Experience social value

Subsequent chapters will examine ways in which the behaviour of staff can be more specifically influenced. The present chapter serves as something of a bridge. It is about ways in which motivations can be

primed
activated
brought to the forefront

for staff during the working day (or night).

These methods are not alternatives to the approaches described earlier—they are supplements. Indeed they could not hope to be effective unless those more strategic approaches were already in use. However,

➤ Human actions are influenced by many factors
➤ Many motivations can be present at any one moment in time

The present chapter considers how to keep the motivations most relevant to quality work as the most powerful influence over what staff do.

WORK SYSTEMS TO PRIME MOTIVATION

There are a number of work practices that will help to keep important motivations salient.

House Rules

These are work procedures and norms that will actively support key motivations. Examples include

Strengths Before Needs

This is a rule that when formal discussions about a service user take place the strengths of the service user will always be presented before any discussion of problems. Strengths include

➤   What the person has achieved
➤   What she enjoys/likes
➤   Positive personal characteristics
➤   People who feel particularly supportive of the individual

Adopting a 'strengths before needs' rule will emphasise the positive aspects of a service user. This will support both help and achievement oriented motivations. It will also counter negative motivations that are built up by rehearsal of problems and difficulties. An exclusive focus on problems may serve to

strengthen feelings of anxiety, anger or hopelessness

The motivations thus engaged will be counterproductive in terms of quality work with the individual. This rule is not about concealing or denying difficulties but about putting them into a realistic perspective.

Compare your own response to the following statements:

Billy bites people severely. He is very strong and unpredictable and has inflicted a number of severe injuries upon staff. He is incontinent, cannot speak and has minimal self care skills. He is a loner, preferring his own company unless there is something that he wants when he will drag you around to show you what he is after. He understands much more than he lets on and is quite manipulative in this respect, choosing who he will and will not respond to.

Billy enjoys walks and swimming. He uses a lot of space and needs time to get used to people being close to him. He can help with washing and dressing but is not yet fully independent. He can feed himself with a spoon or fork and will sometimes use the toilet but is not always continent. He can lead you to things that he wants and understands everyday instructions if the language is simple, gestures are used and he is given time to respond. He sometimes becomes very agitated and will on occasions bite those who are nearby. Sometimes it is clear what has upset him, but not always. There have been two such incidents in the last month.

The information content is very similar, the motivational impact very different.

Some services make the strengths needs rule even more specific by putting numbers on the ratio of strengths to needs—a common ratio is three strengths for every need.

The above example also illustrates a number of other useful house rules.

Describe Don't Evaluate

The language used has other important effects upon the motivations attached to working with particular individuals. It is important that

> the language used about an individual should focus upon accurate description of what is and is not the case rather than upon evaluation of the person, particularly negative evaluation.

In the above example words like unpredictable, minimal, drag, manipulative all carry a negative evaluation of the person and serve to strengthen motivations that run counter to quality work. They suggest that Billy is a person who

➤ Makes little progress
➤ Is unreachable
➤ Is dangerous
➤ Is intentionally difficult

This does not exactly inspire positive motivations for working with Billy.

Positive evaluations can of course have the opposite effect but are more likely to have this impact if the evaluation can be linked to agreed facts (descriptions). Just stating that Billy is likeable and challenging has less impact than a link between these evaluations and facts that everybody knows about Billy.

Describe Situations Don't Ascribe Characteristics

Another language issue relates particularly to how behavioural difficulties are described. Going back to the above example, there is a difference between saying that

> Billy is unpredictable

and

> The reasons for Billy's behaviour are not always obvious to others

> Billy is manipulative

and

> Billy's response to instructions does vary

In the first statements Billy's behaviour is seen to be a function of personal characteristics that he has (unpredictability, manipulativeness). In everyday psychology, personal characteristics are generally viewed as unchangeable. If Billy's behaviour is caused by such characteristics it is therefore unchangeable.

In the second statements, the reasons for Billy's behaviour are left open. This encourages further enquiry and leaves open the possibility of effecting change.

If these kinds of language rules are established as work norms they have an important influence upon staff motivations. They support and make salient motivations relevant to good quality work.

Data not Dogma

The fourth house rule relevant to motivation is that

> decisions on work with service users should be based upon objective information not subjective impressions

It is important to have accurate information on whether

➤ Problematic behaviours are occurring more or less frequently
➤ Skill functioning is better, worse or unchanged
➤ Experiences have or have not occurred

This kind of information requires the observation and recording of behaviour and events. Such information is far more useful than global impressions of whether somebody is 'better' or 'worse'. All too often decisions about people who are unable or who are not allowed to speak for themselves are made upon the basis of subjective impressions.

The issue is not just about accuracy. An emphasis upon objective information stresses that the work is about real world attainment:

➤ Promoting positive change (for example, gain in skills, experiences, well being)
➤ Preventing or limiting negative change (for example, loss of skills)
➤ Maintaining a given situation (for example, current skills or lifestyle)

Information systems therefore help to keep salient achievement oriented motivations.

Supportive Materials

There are a number of ways in which key motivations can be primed by materials available in the work environment. These include

Indirect Supports

Mention was made in Chapter 3 of the use of

> posters
> slogans
> symbols
> available reading materials

as a means of reinforcing key aspects of the service mission. These will prime motivations related to the underlying values of a service.

It would be possible to think of using materials to prime other motivations—for example in relation to social appreciation or career development. The key messages here would be

➤ What we do at work is appreciated by others
➤ What we do at work helps us to learn about ourselves and to achieve other personally relevant goals

This may involve the planned introduction of motivational materials. However, it is also important to review the materials currently available from a motivational perspective. What is the message coming from the materials on the notice board, the papers circulated for meetings? If problems, dangers and negative instructions predominate then this is not supportive of the kinds of motivations relevant to quality helping work.

These are not 'once and for all' interventions. People habituate to materials and priming effects are relatively short lived. It is therefore a matter of regularly reviewing this aspect and looking for new, attention getting ways of conveying motivational messages.

Direct Systems

There are more direct and conscious ways of supporting key motivations. Larger organisations will often have some form of in-house newsletter. This will usually be a means of communicating information. However, its motivational significance should not be overlooked. Stories about

> good quality pieces of work
> achievements by staff and service users
> career development moves
> awards
> 'then' and 'now'

all serve to prime motivations as well as to convey information.

INTERACTIONAL APPROACHES

There are a number of ways in which a manager can fire up staff motivation in the course of face to face interaction:

Reminiscence

Directly recalling or prompting staff to recall

> previous situations compared to now
> successful pieces of work
> appreciations received

is a way of promoting key motivations. Conscious memory is short and service life is often dominated by problems and difficulties. Successes and appreciations are often unavailable to awareness. Story telling and reminding are useful ways of bringing positive motivations to the fore. Such reminiscence may be used in the context of formal discussions or during more informal interactions.

Exhortation

Using handovers and briefings to bring to mind

the service mission
core values
the things that you as a manager appreciate
upcoming positive events
recent achievements

are all means of bringing key motivations to the forefront of the staff's minds. It is a means of psyching up familiar to sports coaches but has a place in human service work. Enthusiasm and a 'go for it' mentality are essential ingredients when tackling complex problems for which there is no ready made, guaranteed solution. Much human service work is of this nature.

CONCLUSIONS

Previous chapters have identified strategic ways of managing a workplace to generate and support the motivations that underpin good quality human service work. The impact of these approaches can be enhanced if thought is given to ways of bringing motivation to life on a day to day basis. The ideas contained in this chapter are complementary to, not an alternative for, the longer range interventions. However, given the complex and often chaotic nature of human motivation and behaviour their importance should not be underestimated.

SUMMARY

1. IT IS IMPORTANT TO BRING KEY MOTIVATIONS TO THE FORE-FRONT OF STAFF'S MINDS SO THAT THEY EXERT THE GREATEST POSSIBLE INFLUENCE OVER MOMENT TO MOMENT FUNCTIONING AT WORK.

2. THIS CAN BE EFFECTED BY SETTING NORMS AT WORK WHICH ALL STAFF ARE EXPECTED TO FOLLOW. EXAMPLES OF SUCH NORMS INCLUDE
   A. A FOCUS ON POSITIVE ASPECTS OF A SERVICE USER IN ANY DISCUSSION OF DIFFICULT OR PROBLEMATIC ASPECTS (STRENGTHS BEFORE NEEDS)
   B. INSISTING ON THE LANGUAGE USED ABOUT OTHERS BEING DESCRIPTIVE RATHER THAN EVALUATIVE (DESCRIBE DON'T EVALUATE)
   C. INSISTING THAT LANGUAGE BE USED TO DESCRIBE SITUATIONS RATHER THAN TO ATTRIBUTE BEHAVIOUR TO PERSONAL CHARACTERISTICS (DESCRIBE SITUATIONS DON'T ASCRIBE CHARACTERISTICS)
   D. DEVELOPING SYSTEMS SO THAT DECISIONS ARE BASED UPON OBJECTIVE INFORMATION RATHER THAN SUBJECTIVE IMPRESSIONS (DATA NOT DOGMA)

3. THE VERBAL AND PICTORIAL MATERIALS AVAILABLE IN THE WORK ENVIRONMENT WILL INFLUENCE THE MOTIVATIONS

EXPERIENCED BY STAFF. CURRENTLY AVAILABLE MATERIALS SHOULD BE REVIEWED FROM A MOTIVATIONAL PERSPECTIVE AND THE USE OF SPECIFIC ADDITIONAL MATERIALS CAN BE CONSIDERED.

4. FACE TO FACE INTERACTIONS WITH STAFF CAN BE USED TO MOTIVATIONAL EFFECT. TACTICS INCLUDE RECALL OF PAST SUCCESSES, PROGRESS OVER TIME, FORTHCOMING POSITIVE EVENTS; AND DIRECT REMINDERS ABOUT THE CORE VALUES AND PURPOSES OF A SERVICE.

Manager's toolkit	
Tools	Applications
Set group norms	Promote relevant motivations
Model	Show norms in action
Establish information systems	Generate accurate/objective information on service and user functioning
Analyse/develop the verbal and pictorial materials around the work environment	Support key motivational messages
Question	Aid recall of past successes, change over time, appreciations received, future positives
State	Directly evoking past successes, change over time, appreciations, future positives, core values and purposes of service
Give feedback	Encourage constructive ways of talking about users. Discourage unhelpful ways of talking about users

SECTION III

Creating and Sustaining Performance

This section looks at the factors which exert a direct influence over what staff do (their ACTIONS, in STAR model terms).

Chapter 9 considers these ACTIONS themselves.

Actions . . . are the behaviours that the individual carries out in order to satisfy salient wants and needs. They are the means of coping with the motivations experienced, achieving the desired positive outcomes, escaping from or avoiding important negative outcomes. In terms of this book the key actions are those that constitute good quality work.

Chapter 10 considers TRIGGERS as sources of information

> **Triggers . . . are events (internal or external) that immediately pre-cede action. They trigger behaviour. Triggers operate by**
>
> **Reflex . . . Priming motivation . . . Providing information**
>
> **Although triggers serve rather different functions the thing that they have in common is that they occur close in time to behaviour and predict the fact that a behaviour is likely to occur.**

Chapters 11 to 14 consider RESULTS as an important determinant of what staff continue to do, the ACTIONS that they sustain.

> **Results . . . are the events that . . . follow**
> **Actions . . . and . . . influence whether particular actions are repeated.**
>
> **Actions will continue in so far as they lead to the satisfaction of important motivations. Such satisfaction may be based upon**
>
> **a.   Positive reinforcement . . . an Action is likely to be repeated in so far as it achieves something that the individual positively desires.**
>
> **b.   Negative reinforcement . . . an Action is likely to be repeated in so far as the individual escapes from or avoids unpleasant experiences.**
>
> **c.   Extinction . . . an Action becomes less likely if it achieves nothing of importance to the individual.**
>
> **d.   Punishment . . . an Action becomes less likely if it is consistently followed by something aversive.**
>
> **e.   Differential reinforcement . . . over time Actions will be shaped towards those that achieve the 'best' Results. Where one behaviour achieves better results than another more time will be spent on that behaviour.**

CHAPTER 9   It would help if I knew

AIMS OF THE CHAPTER

1. To discuss the role of training in developing staff motivation and on the job competence.

2. To articulate those areas of staff functioning that can be influenced by training.

3. To identify the factors which determine the effectiveness of training inputs.

INTRODUCTION

In human service settings there seems often to be the (unspoken) assumption that everyone knows how to do the job of helping and caring.

➤ Most of the staff in such services have no formal qualifications
➤ Selection procedures rarely focus on the current skills of applicants
➤ Little training is offered once people are in post

The message of this is clear

anyone and everyone knows how to help other human beings who have complex long term disabilities

I am not sure that many of the readers of this book would appreciate it if such an attitude prevailed in, for example, acute medical services!

This 'message' derives from the low status of people with long term disabilities, whether these are to do with mental health, old age, physical functioning or learning and development.

It is important not to mistake this question of social value for the truth.

Quality work with people who have such difficulties is highly skilled and is far more than doing 'what comes naturally'.

WHAT IS TRAINING?

This is not the book for deep philosophical discussions! For present purposes training refers to any systematic attempt to influence the knowledge, skills and values of staff

The ways in which this is done will vary—for example

➤   Off site courses
➤   On site courses
➤   Brief training sessions in the working day
➤   On the job modelling and coaching
➤   Personal study

Training thus incorporates a range of activities, not just formally constituted training courses.

WHY TRAIN

Training can help to sustain and develop work relevant motivations. As outlined in Chapter 6 a systematic approach to training can

> create an 'educational climate'

which

> enhances motivations such as curiosity, the wish to know, to learn, to develop as an individual

These motivations 'fit' well with quality work in human services.

However, motivation is not enough. In order to ensure good quality work performance staff need to

➤   Understand exactly what is required of them
➤   Be capable of carrying out the necessary actions

Training is a way to help people carry out their work effectively. It is not the only way. It is not necessarily the best way. There can be very little carryover from training to on the job functioning. All the other factors outlined in this book need to be addressed if quality work is to be implemented and sustained.

Training has an important but limited influence on staff performance.

WHAT TO TRAIN

There are three areas of staff functioning which are open to influence by training: skills, knowledge and values.

Skills (Actions)

Training can be a means of influencing what staff do at work—how they act and react in relation to service users. From lifting to listening, staff need to learn the specific skills which go to make up competence at work.

Knowledge

This is a more abstract level than skills and will be mainly revealed in what staff think and say in relation to their work. It covers

➤ General information about service users and their needs
➤ Why certain skills are important (the rationale, the theories)

Knowledge and skills are not directly related—a staff member can be very skilful without being knowledgeable or very knowledgeable without being skilful. However, it is generally felt that giving people knowledge in addition to skills enables them to

➤ Act in a more flexible way
➤ Judge better how to initiate or respond to situations
➤ Develop more innovatory approaches
➤ Present a better picture of service functioning

Values

The question as to 'why we do what we do?' can be answered at two levels.

1. Based upon knowledge of the physical universe and its rules of operation—the scientific or technical answer.
2. Based upon the moral universe, the world of values, good and bad, right and wrong.

Human action is intimately linked to human values. In the discussion on service mission (Chapter 3) the role of the values underpinning a service was emphasised. They

➤ Provide the rationale for a service
➤ Give it human meaning

Values also tend to have a strong emotional component—they provide both the abstract rationale and the fire for action. They ENERGISE.

Training is often seen as an important vehicle for

➤ Conveying to staff the values that underpin a service
➤ Influencing staff values
➤ Giving the moral answer to the question 'why?'

Thus training activities will target skills, knowledge and values and all three areas are seen as important influences upon how staff behave on a day to day basis.

Who Decides on the Content of Training

Training for job performance (which is what this chapter is about) will obviously be determined by the

skills, knowledge and values necessary for good quality work

Thus at one level the employer determines the content of training. However, it is important to look for ways of engaging staff in the process of determining what is to be learned, to give staff some influence over the content of training:

➤ The more actively that the learner is involved in the training process the more likely it is that learning will occur
➤ Staff will have more intimate knowledge of the job in practice and their own learning needs so that training can be directed more efficiently
➤ Consultation demonstrates respect for staff, an important support to motivation in general

Thus what goes into training will be

     skills   knowledge   values

The precise content should be determined by

➤ Job requirements
➤ An analysis of the current competence of the individual staff member
➤ Staff preference

HOW TO TRAIN

This is a topic worthy of a book in itself. However, attention will be drawn to basic issues which play an important part in determining whether training is effective in changing skills, knowledge and values. These issues include

Learner Involvement

There is a general principle that learning of any kind is enhanced by the active involvement of the learner. Passively receiving information is not a good recipe for change. Active involvement includes

➤ The learner having some say over the content of training
➤ Participation in the training process itself

Clearly some information has to be presented. However, this needs to be supplemented by learner activity which goes beyond watching and listening—for example

➤ Asking and answering questions
➤ Discussing topics
➤ Solving presented problems
➤ Making plans
➤ Carrying out assignments

Effective training will be participative.

The Training Medium

Verbal presentation will influence verbal behaviour. Motor presentation will influence motor behaviour.

If skills are the target of training it is vital that the training process involve actual practice of the skills in question. This may involve

➤ Demonstration
➤ Role play
➤ Practice in the actual work situation

Any such practice element is in turn enhanced by

feedback on performance

Thus effective skills training must contain

demonstration, practice and feedback elements

Knowledge tends to be verbally encoded and knowledge training will contain a stronger verbal element.

Values training is an interesting area because whilst it has a strong verbal component, values are often linked to emotions such as joy, guilt, anger.

Values training is therefore likely to need a strong emotional element to it. This may be effected by

➤ Powerful visual images
➤ Telling anecdotes
➤ Witness accounts
➤ Practical exercises such as going through the same experiences as the people who are the users of human services

Thus the medium of training needs to fit the target of training and any mismatch will reduce the effectiveness of the training input.

The Training Environment

There are two major principles here. One is that

change is most likely when what is presented is attended to without distraction

Anything that creates distraction will reduce the effectiveness of training. This will include factors such as

➤ Heating
➤ Lighting
➤ Seating
➤ Intrusions (e.g. telephone or pager)
➤ Behaviour of the presenter (e.g. distracting habits, use of jargon)

The second key principle is that

> extremes of arousal—high or low—will impair learning

Anything that creates extremes of arousal during the training process will reduce the effectiveness of training. This will include factors such as

➤ Evoking extreme anxiety or anger in participants
➤ Physical climate variables (as above)
➤ Monotonous presentation techniques
➤ The availability of alcohol during training

Time of day can also be a consideration in that alertness does vary across the day. There are a lot of individual differences in this—different people having peaks at different times (larks and owls). However, a popular view is that learning is better in the first half of the day.

The Packaging of Information

There are three important points here

1. People's concentration span when passively engaged in watching or listening should not be assumed to be much more than 20 minutes.
2. There is a limit to the number of new items of information, key points that can be taken on board at any one time (three to five items being a crude guide).
3. Repetition enhances learning.

Thus effective training will

➤ Present a limited number of key points at any one time
➤ Go over these more than once
➤ Use short stretches of passive involvement

The Social Aspects of Training

Everyone differs in their speed and style of learning. In theory a completely individual approach—the learner working individually with the tutor (human, book or electronic device)—is ideal. However, this

➤ Might be uncomfortable for some individuals
➤ Misses out on some of the advantages of learning with others

These advantages include

➤ The chance to learn from each other, not just the tutor
➤ The facilitation of practicum elements such as role play
➤ The motivational elements of group work (be it competition or mutual support)

There are clearly limits on group size if all members of the group are required to develop targeted skills, knowledge and values. As a rough guide when group numbers move above 10–12 it becomes difficult for a human tutor to keep close contact with all students and to ensure that all reach the training targets.

Distilling from the above, effective training will

- ➤ Be participative
- ➤ Be individualised
- ➤ Contain demonstration, practice and feedback elements when skills are the training target
- ➤ Contain emotional elements when values are the training target
- ➤ Be delivered in manageable chunks, in distraction free environments, at optimum levels of arousal
- ➤ Be organised on an individual or small group basis

There may be many good reasons why we assemble large groups of people and talk at them over long periods of time.

- ➤ Economic reasons
  - – to achieve maximum spread in terms of numbers from limited training resources
  - – to achieve for trainers maximum return for minimum work
- ➤ Social reasons
  - – the benefits of meeting and chatting with others away from the immediate pressures of work (networking)
  - – the pleasure of the paid awayday

However, these reasons, good though they are, must be distinguished from having anything to do with the utility of training as a means of effecting change in the skills, knowledge and values of staff.

WHEN TO TRAIN

For training to impact upon performance it is important that

the skills, knowledge and values trained have immediate relevance

Training should focus upon those aspects of performance that are required for high quality everyday work. If staff find themselves having to confront issues, deal with problems, for which they do not have the competence this will

- ➤ Put them under a great deal of pressure
- ➤ Raise the likelihood of avoidance behaviours
- ➤ Raise the likelihood of 'bad habits' developing

If on the other hand staff are trained in competences for which there is no immediate requirement in their everyday work then the knowledge and skills trained will

- ➤ Not become consolidated
- ➤ Tend to decline over time

Thus the most effective training will be delivered 'just in time'—be closely tied to the current competences required of staff.

These competences themselves are not static.

➤   Staff may change role
➤   A service may develop new standards in relation to consumer pressure
➤   A service may develop new standards in relation to advances in knowledge

Evolving staff performance requires evolving training inputs.

DELIVERING TRAINING

The considerations of timing, when taken in conjunction with the points made in the previous section on training methods, suggest that

> the traditional training format of assembling large groups together and running courses is not ideal

With staff turning over and standards evolving continuously, there is an ongoing need for training activity. This may be met by

1.   Repeated training courses to which ready access can be gained. The logistics of this are formidable, particularly in relation to smaller service providing agencies.
2.   More self managed, open approaches to training. This enables staff to take up training on a more flexible basis. It too requires serious logistical consideration but of a rather different sort. It is far more than sending a staff member off to watch a video or to read some text. It requires carefully planned:

     –   multimedia materials
     –   linked practical assignments
     –   tutor supervision

Whilst there are many excellent models of open learning, their application to the everyday work of human services engaged with people who have serious long term disabilities is relatively underdeveloped.

WHO TRAINS

The key requirements are that

➤   The content of the training reflects the competences targeted
➤   The training be delivered in an effective way (see above)

The training itself may be carried out by

➤   A manager
➤   An individual within an agency with specific training responsibilities
➤   An individual from outside an agency with specific training responsibilities
➤   The staff member, on a more self managed basis

However, open, more self directed approaches do not preclude the need for a human tutor. The human tutor retains a vital role in

organising
supporting
encouraging
clarifying
supervising

the learning process so that

targeted outcomes are achieved

The question of whether to use in-house or external personnel in training will in part reflect practical considerations, such as the availability within an agency of

➤ Time
➤ Money
➤ Expertise

There is also the concept of the 'outsider effect'—that a message delivered by someone not involved in an agency may have far more impact than the same message delivered by someone with whom staff are familiar on a day to day basis. If this effect is real then it may be of greatest use when a service and its staff

➤ Need to develop new standards, new competences

and

➤ No headway has been made with in-house resources

Overreliance on charismatic outsiders may produce high levels of enjoyment and satisfaction but in the long run may be detrimental to an agency as it can undermine the credibility of in-house resources and of the agency management in general.

CONCLUSIONS

For staff to function effectively on a day to day basis, to act in ways that are defined as high quality, they have to possess the appropriate skills, knowledge and values. Training is a means of providing them with the competences that they lack. This requires that those competences are clearly defined and staff accurately assessed in terms of their possession of these competences. Once training needs are identified then the gaps can be filled by appropriate training inputs. In theory training can be a powerful aid to performance. However, its impact can be readily undermined if close attention is not paid to why, when and how it is provided.

SUMMARY

1. TRAINING IS ANY SYSTEMATIC ATTEMPT TO INFLUENCE THE SKILLS, KNOWLEDGE AND VALUES OF STAFF.

2. TRAINING CAN ENHANCE GENERAL MOTIVATIONS AS WELL AS SPECIFIC AREAS OF STAFF COMPETENCE.

3. TRAINING NEEDS SHOULD BE DETERMINED BY JOB ANALYSIS AND CONSULTATION WITH STAFF.

4. TRAINING IS MOST LIKELY TO BE EFFECTIVE IF IT

   – IS PARTICIPATIVE
   – IS INDIVIDUALISED
   – CONTAINS DEMONSTRATION, PRACTICE AND FEEDBACK ELEMENTS WHEN SKILLS ARE THE TRAINING TARGET
   – CONTAINS EMOTIONAL ELEMENTS WHEN VALUES ARE THE TRAINING TARGET
   – IS DELIVERED IN MANAGEABLE CHUNKS, IN DISTRACTION FREE ENVIRONMENTS AT OPTIMUM LEVELS OF AROUSAL
   – IS ORGANISED ON AN INDIVIDUAL OR SMALL GROUP BASIS
   – IS DELIVERED CLOSE IN TIME TO WHEN THE TARGETED KNOWLEDGE, SKILLS AND VALUES ARE REQUIRED IN EVERYDAY WORK

5. THE DELIVERY OR SUPERVISION OF TRAINING SHOULD BE DETERMINED BY COMPETENCE AS WELL AS PRACTICAL CONSIDERATIONS SUCH AS AVAILABILITY.

6. THERE IS A NEED TO DEVELOP A WIDER RANGE OF OPEN LEARNING SYSTEMS FOR USE IN HUMAN SERVICES.

Manager's toolkit	
Tools	Applications
Job analysis	Identify skills, knowledge and values required by staff
Questioning	Identify current knowledge and values of staff and learning preferences
Observation	Identify current skills of staff
Listening	Identify personal learning preferences of staff
Modelling	Influence staff competence
Feedback	Influence staff competence
Presentation	Influence staff knowledge and values
Problem solving	Match training inputs to training needs

CHAPTER 10   Remember . . . remember

AIMS OF THE CHAPTER

1. To OUTLINE PROCEDURES FOR ORGANISING TIME IN THE WORKPLACE.

2. To CONSIDER METHODS FOR TRIGGERING APPROPRIATE STAFF ACTIONS.

INTRODUCTION

The previous *section* concentrated upon strategies for

> creating
> strengthening
> priming

a range of motivations relevant to both

> job performance

and

> job satisfaction

The previous *chapter* looked at ways of ensuring that staff have the necessary competences to carry out effectively the work that is asked of them.

These are both *necessary* conditions for good functioning at work. However, they may not be *sufficient* to guarantee adequate performance on a day to day, moment to moment basis. The present chapter, and those that follow in the section, look at these more micro level influences on actual service delivery.

THE NATURE OF THE WORKLOAD

In care services the work of front line staff involves a variety of tasks—tasks relating to

> The care of the clients
> The functioning of the team
> The service of which the team is a part
> Personal development (staff)

A bewildering array which can easily result in conflicting priorities and general overload.

To make matters even more complex . . .

In each area—client support, team functioning, organisational functioning, personal development—there will be

➤ Tasks which are related to long term goals (for example, teaching an individual to manage her own money in order that she may live unsupported in the community)
➤ Tasks which are related to more immediate everyday matters (for example, helping clients to get ready for work/day centre)

In addition there will be

➤ Unexpected crises which also require attention (for example taking a client to the doctor, helping a client change out of wet clothes, reassuring a client who has become distressed)

In many care settings staff functioning can be almost entirely reactive—responding to crises or events as they happen.

Thus care work is

➤ Complex
➤ Multifaceted
➤ Often pressured

Without careful planning it is quite understandable that staff members carry out the tasks which are

➤ Simplest
➤ Quickest
➤ Demanding of the most immediate attention

When day to day work is conducted in this manner

➤ More important but longer term tasks relating to the team's 'mission' may never get started at all or, if started, may not get completed
➤ The whole service may drift and lose its sense of purpose and direction

The task of the manager therefore goes beyond getting staff motivated and skilled. Giving staff the STAR treatment also includes getting them to

➤ Allocate time to tasks in accordance with their overall priority
➤ Do the appropriate tasks at the appropriate time

ORGANISING THE WORKLOAD

Organising the workload efficiently requires attention to both long and short term goals in addition to daily routines and unexpected disruptions or crises. It involves

➤ Setting priorities
➤ Setting short term goals and targets
➤ Organising each week/day
➤ Providing reminders/cues for specific actions

Setting Priorities

Work priorities must relate directly to the

➤ Overall mission of the organisation and team
➤ Specific objectives that derive from the mission

Example

An organisation's mission may be to help people with chronic psychiatric illness lead a fulfilling life in the community, using methods which at all times show respect and value for the individual. The objectives that arise from this 'mission' include

- helping people to develop the skills required to live independently
- training staff in appropriate interpersonal skills which reflect value and respect for the individual despite sometimes very difficult behaviour by that individual
- enabling the staff team to provide a coordinated and consistent service to their clients
- helping staff to develop their own skills and knowledge of working with clients who have chronic psychiatric illness

The exact tasks that follow from these objectives depend upon the individual needs of clients, staff and the working team.

Setting, monitoring and reviewing priorities requires the presence of a range of organisational structures and systems:

Individual programme planning. To define and review individual client priorities on an annual or six monthly basis.

Appraisal (individual performance review). To define and review individual staff priorities.

Team analysis. To define and review team functioning and team priorities on an annual or six monthly basis.

In all these areas the manager needs to be alert to the

➤ Number of goals being set
➤ Level of priority being assigned (see later)

It is all too easy for staff to become overwhelmed by

➤ The absolute number of tasks/goals set (see Chapter 5)
➤ The failure to order goals in terms of priority

However, the presence of clear goals/targets is a powerful trigger for action.

Setting Short Term Goals and Targets

Whilst longer term goals and targets do act as a trigger they may seem rather unattainable and the time span itself can be so long as to remove any sense of urgency about tackling the priorities. It is therefore important that the longer term goals are

> broken down into smaller tasks

with

> dates set for review/completion

Example

Longer term goal:
Jim will be helped to find a job

Short term targets:
1. Discuss with Jim the types of job that he wants to do (before January 31st)
2. Check if Jim has the qualifications for the job (by February 28th)
3. Practise job interview skills (start March)
4. Find out where to apply for the relevant jobs (by March 7th)
5. Apply for jobs (March onwards)
6. Prepare for specific interviews (as appropriate)

As for setting priorities (see above) the process of breaking down longer term goals into shorter term targets is helped by the presence of a number of organisational structures/systems. These include

➤ Staff supervision sessions
➤ Regular team meetings
➤ Regular client review meetings
➤ Regular personal review sessions

Each of these structures has in common

➤ Allocating a specific and regular time for establishing short term goals and targets
➤ Identifying the specific tasks which need to be undertaken and the specific person who will take responsibility for these tasks, if the short term goal is to be accomplished
➤ Setting a date for the completion/review of the tasks decided upon

Example

Long term goal:
Jim will be helped to find a job

Short term target:
Discuss with Jim the types of job that he wants to do (before January 31st)

Tasks
1. Get a book from the library on jobs and careers
2. Go through with Jim the various job possibilities to narrow down his interests
3. Get more information about the jobs on Jim's short list
4. Discuss with Jim

An important point to note is that

> tasks are more likely to be completed if a date is set for completion/review

Organising Each Week/Day

Planning is needed in order to ensure that time is allocated in a week/day to all aspects of service work:

- Work directed towards long term goals
- Routine tasks
- Crises

Each week a specific time should be allocated to establishing priorities for the coming week. This will outline how time will be apportioned between

- Routine tasks
- Longer term work

Each day time should be allocated to planning that day. This should be rather more detailed:

1. Tasks for the day are listed out.
2. Each task is given a priority rating.
   A = most important and most urgent
   B = most important but less urgent
   C = not important but urgent
   D = not important and not urgent
3. Time is allocated to tasks according to their importance and urgency.
4. Extra time needs to be left for unexpected crises.
5. Named people are delegated to accomplishing each task.
6. The daily list of things to do is posted up for all to see.
7. As each task is accomplished it is marked off the list.

If possible time should be given at the end of the day to reviewing how the day has gone.

It may be felt that this is all too bureaucratic. However, it cannot be emphasised STRONGLY enough that

> unless care is taken to manage time effectively, important but non-urgent tasks will be swept aside by the pressure of events and moment to moment personal inclinations

Providing Reminders/Cues for Specific Actions

There are many triggers for appropriate work actions which can be made salient and effective in the workplace. These include

Verbal Reminders from the Manager

Reminding a staff member to carry out a task is an obvious and often effective trigger. Such cueing is enhanced if the reminder includes a link between

> doing the task

and

> a positive outcome (for the client, the staff member, the team or the service)

This will help to generate work relevant motivations. The alternative—reminding of the negative consequences if the task is not carried out—is less helpful as it may generate anger/anxiety motivations which are not in general supportive of quality work in care services. However, sometimes . . .

Visual Presence of the Manager

Mere presence will trigger action if the staff member links this to likely results

If she sees me doing a good job something positive may happen.
If she sees me not working something negative may happen.

These links depend upon the staff's previous experience with the manager. However, this point does strengthen one of the general messages of this book:

> care services need hands on, visible management

Manager Modelling the Task

Seeing the manager getting on with a task may act as a reminder to staff that they should be doing this themselves. Modelling is a powerful trigger as it can

> Demonstrate what to do (helpful for staff who are not sure/not confident)
> Show the link between the action and a positive result

Example

The manager comes into the lounge where residents are sitting around doing nothing. As she engages them in conversation or sets up an activity she not only reminds the staff, who are engrossed in a television programme, that they should be paying attention to the residents but also demonstrates the positive benefits for the residents of being occupied and engaged.

Symbolic Presence of the Manager

Memos and written instructions can trigger appropriate work actions if

➤ There are not too many of them
➤ They do not occur too often
➤ They carry information about the positive results that will be achieved by completing the task

To-do Lists

These lists—mentioned earlier—are powerful triggers for completion of daily tasks/ activities. The previous example was of a general list for the team. However, this can be made more powerful if each staff member makes a personal to-do list for the day or week. As before, prioritising tasks using symbols or letters will help to ensure that the most important tasks are completed.

Timetables

Timetables are to-do lists with additional information. They can include

➤ The time when a task is to be done
➤ The place where a task is to be done
➤ The staff designated to the task

They can incorporate the work schedules across the whole staff group/team.

Databases

A database can be helpful in triggering actions in a number of ways. Databases come in various forms—checklists, card indexes, directories, computerised formats. They act as a source of information and thereby a reminder of what to do.

Examples

Staff seeking to expand a client's range of leisure activities will be helped by a directory of local resources.

Staff who are finding it hard to teach a client a particular skill will be more likely to persevere if they can access a card index containing ideas on how to teach specific skills.

Providing a client with a range of activities will be helped if there is a checklist of activities that the individual enjoys. Space can be provided alongside the name of each activity to enter the date/ time when the activity was carried out. In this way staff can have rapid access to information which provides a useful cue as to what to do *now*.

Written Programme Plans

A written programme is more likely to be carried out than one that is not written. The written programme acts as a

➤ General reminder to carry out the task
➤ Specific reminder as to how, when and where the task is to be carried out

If possible posting the programme up increases its salience and its power to trigger action.

Similar considerations apply to recording charts where the work of the staff is to record particular behaviours as and when they occur.

> a well structured recording system

linked to

> a reason for doing the recording

with

> charts prominently displayed or easily accessible

raises the likelihood of staff actually carrying out the recording.

Verbal Commitment

If an individual makes a public commitment to carry out a task this raises the likelihood that the task will be completed.

Setting Review Dates

As mentioned earlier a task with a review date is more likely to be carried out than one without. However, this form of triggering will only be effective if

> there is a functioning review system

If review dates are not meaningful—they get forgotten, are not adhered to—then setting a date will not act as a trigger. With a functioning system it will . . . and its power can be enhanced if the date is made salient (for example writing it in to diaries, calendars, timetables).

These approaches to triggering are very much concerned with ensuring that the more variable and individualised tasks are carried out. They are an essential part of translating good ideas into everyday life and practice. Of course work also includes a number of more mundane, invariant tasks. This is where the notion of routine comes in useful:

> triggering by habit

If a task is always carried out

at the same time

or

always follows a specific previous activity

then the time or previous activity come to trigger the action.

Examples

If washing up is always done straight after the meal then the meal ending triggers washing up without need for any other triggering device.

If paperwork or other administrative tasks are allocated a particular time or place in a sequence (the half hour after residents have gone off to day provision) then the tasks get done and do not intrude at other times.

EVALUATING THE USE OF TIME

Given that time is one of the key resources in delivering a quality service, evaluating its use is a key managerial activity. Such evaluation can be done at two levels:

A General but Informal Review of Day to Day Life

This may indicate a number of things that absorb time but have no/limited relevance to the real work of the service. Common time wasters include

➤ Meetings starting/finishing later than their agreed times
➤ People popping in for a chat
➤ Non-urgent phone calls
➤ Visitors

Taking steps to control these influences will make an important contribution to there being time for important work tasks.

A Formal Analysis of Time Allocations

It will be useful every so often for the team to evaluate in detail how time is being spent. This requires use of an activity time log (Table 10.1).

Table 10.1   Sample procedure for analysing use of time

1. The staff team makes a list of the team's priorities and tasks
2. Each staff member keeps a daily log of everything they do and the time taken to do it (minimum time a week)
3. The logs are analysed—each activity is listed and the time spent on it calculated
4. The comparison is made between the way the team thinks that time should be spent and the way that it is actually being spent
5. If there is a mismatch, problem solving is undertaken to resolve this

Time is a vital resource but it needs active management if it is to be used to best advantage.

CONCLUSIONS

Day to day service work will be strongly influenced by the immediate pressures in the environment. It is important to ensure that the longer term aspects of quality work feature as salient in this respect. However, this requires analysis, planning and structuring of that most vital resource—time.

SUMMARY

1. CARE WORK IS COMPLEX AND MULTIFACETED.

2. CREATING AND STRENGTHENING THE MOTIVATION OF STAFF IS NOT ALWAYS ENOUGH TO GUARANTEE GOOD PERFORMANCE ON A DAY TO DAY BASIS.

3. IT IS EASY FOR CARE WORK TO BECOME ENTIRELY REACTIVE.

4. IN ORDER TO FACILITATE GOOD FUNCTIONING STAFF'S TIME NEEDS TO BE WELL ORGANISED.

5. ORGANISING TIME NEEDS REFERENCE TO THE SERVICE MISSION AND THE PRIORITIES THAT IT INDICATES.

6. DAY TO DAY TIME NEEDS TO BE ORGANISED TO ENSURE THAT SPACE IS AVAILABLE FOR LONGER TERM GOALS AS WELL AS ROUTINE TASKS AND THE CRISES THAT INEVITABLY ARISE IN HUMAN SERVICE WORK.

7. ORGANISING THE WORKLOAD REQUIRES ATTENTION TO SETTING PRIORITIES, SETTING SHORT TERM GOALS, ORGANISING EACH WEEK AND EACH DAY, PROVIDING TRIGGERS FOR SPECIFIC ACTIONS.

8. SETTING PRIORITIES IS SUPPORTED BY SYSTEMS SUCH AS INDIVIDUAL PROGRAMME PLANNING, INDIVIDUAL PERFORMANCE REVIEW, TEAM ANALYSIS.

9. SETTING SHORT TERM GOALS IS SUPPORTED BY SYSTEMS SUCH AS STAFF SUPERVISION, REGULAR TEAM MEETINGS, REGULAR CLIENT REVIEWS, REGULAR PERSONAL REVIEWS.

10. TRIGGERS TO CUE STAFF TO CARRY OUT SPECIFIC ACTIVITIES INCLUDE VERBAL REMINDERS, MANAGERIAL PRESENCE, MODELLING, MEMOS, TO-DO LISTS, TIMETABLES, DATABASES, WRITTEN PROGRAMME PLANS, VERBAL COMMITMENT, SETTING REVIEW DATES.

11. Time and tasks need to be planned on a weekly and a daily basis.

12. Tasks need to be rated in terms of priority.

13. The use of time needs to be kept under review to reduce time wasters and to control for drift of time allocation away from service priorities.

Manager's toolkit	
Tools	Applications
Individual planning systems	Establish priorities in client work. Establish priorities in staff development
Team analysis	Establish priorities in team development
Goal setting	Trigger staff actions
Task analysis	Break longer term goals into short term targets
Individual supervision	Ensure feasible goals are set and monitored
Organising/managing meetings	Ensure feasible goals are set and monitored
Time management	Ensure time is allocated to tasks in relation to their priority. Monitor use of time
Reminding (spoken/written)	Ensure specific tasks done
Being around	Ensure specific tasks done
Modelling	Ensure specific tasks done
Timetabling	Ensure specific tasks done
Establishing databases	Ensure specific tasks done

CHAPTER 11   It's nice to know that I've achieved something

AIMS OF THE CHAPTER

1. To consider the nature and function of effective performance feedback to staff.

2. To outline the content elements of feedback that will promote job performance.

3. To outline ways of collecting and delivering feedback information.

INTRODUCTION

When a staff member makes an effort at work it is important for that individual to know WHAT and HOW MUCH has been achieved. Such information can play a vital role in

improving

and   high quality performance

sustaining

Such information—knowledge of results—can have a number of effects:

➤ It can act as a reinforcer and strengthen aspects of job performance (positive results)
➤ It can extinguish/punish and thereby decrease aspects of job performance (negative results)
➤ It can increase self reliance by enabling the individual to monitor his own performance in relation to agreed/desired standards
➤ It can enhance personal growth by
  – consolidating learning where success is achieved
  – triggering problem solving when desired outcomes are not achieved
➤ It can increase self confidence as the individual understands more accurately the relationship between effort and outcome
➤ It can support and strengthen general achievement motivation

Performance related feedback is relevant to any aspect of work where energy and effort is expended;

➤ Routine tasks
➤ User centred problem solving

➤ Service innovation
➤ Personal development activities

However, regardless of the particular task certain fundamental principles need to be applied if the feedback is to be useful to the individual concerned.

CLARITY IN THE OUTCOMES SOUGHT

Feedback can only be influential if it is clear

what it is that staff are supposed to do

and/or

what results are expected from making the required effort

Comments such as

You're doing ok
You've done well
Not bad
Could be better
You need to pull your socks up

may have a temporary impact upon how the person feels. They will have no effect on specific functioning at work because they do not specify

➤ The staff actions being commented upon
➤ The standards used to make the evaluation

Thus knowledge of results is only possible where expectations are stated clearly in terms of performance:

➤ What staff are actually supposed to do
➤ What observable outcomes are expected as a result of a piece of work

This issue is covered more fully in Chapter 5. However, an additional useful distinction may be made between

performance standards

and

behavioural goals

Performance Standards

There are certain areas of work where it is expected that staff will always achieve a specific standard—it is part of the routine, it is what is expected to always occur. Such expectations need to be defined in terms of behaviours or performances and then the level of performance required is defined in measurable terms (the standard).

Examples

Target: Key worker to maintain contact with family of child in residential school
Performance: Telephone calls to parents
Standard required: One telephone call to family each week

Target: To encourage community integration
Performance: Service user to be taken out to social events by staff
Standard required: two off-site evening activities to be offered each week

Target: To keep house clean
Performance: Vacuuming, dusting, washing down paintwork
Standard required: Carpets vacuumed daily, furniture dusted weekly, paintwork washed down weekly

Target: To show respect to service users
Performance: Speaking respectfully
Standard required: There will be no shouting by staff unless danger is threatened

As can be seen standard setting is another way of specifying clear goals (Chapter 5) but applied to tasks where a given level of performance is always expected. It clarifies

who will do what and to what degree of success

The clarity makes it possible to generate accurate feedback and thereby sustain quality on a routine basis.

Behavioural Goals

This is fully covered in Chapter 5. These are the targets set in relation to

developmental
innovative
problem solving

tasks . . . for the

individual
team

Goals specify

who will do what, to what degree of success and by when

Goals will be long and short term. Again it is the clarity that makes it possible to generate effective feedback.

ATTAINABILITY OF STANDARDS AND GOALS

Again this issue is covered more fully in Chapter 5. It is vital that

the standards and goals set are attainable

Some will be difficult, some will be easy but there must be a good overall chance of success.

if   impossible standards and goals are set
then   knowledge of results, performance feedback will be continually negative

The experience of continual failure will have a damaging effect upon motivation and creates conditions under which active distress can occur (see Chapters 15 and 16). Constructive outcomes from failures are only likely in a context where successes occur at a relatively higher rate.

PRINCIPLES FOR DEVELOPING ACCURATE INFORMATION SYSTEMS

Information may be collected about staff or service user behaviours.

It may be collected by the

➤ Manager
➤ Staff
➤ Service user

Whatever information is collected, by whom, there are a number of important general issues to consider if the information gathered is to be accurate and useful for feedback purposes.

What to Measure

General

Measures should minimise subjective information and focus upon things that are as objective as possible. The most common things to measure are

➤ Observable behaviour—for example, walking, sitting, punching, writing, smiling
➤ The tangible outcome of behaviour—for example, a clean floor, a typed report, a till receipt, a broken window

In some cases it will be necessary for the measure to reflect more subjective variables:

➤ A sensation (for example, pain)
➤ An emotion (for example, anxiety)
➤ A state (for example, satisfaction)

However, with a little thought these subjective elements can be put into some form of scale which enables a judgement to be made with a degree of objectivity.

The Unit of Measurement

The simplest and most useful measures of progress and change are numerical ones. Numerical units are easy to interpret

and

present

There are three common kinds of numerical measures.

1. *Measures of physical dimensions.* The most common such units are

➤ Frequency—the number of occurrences of a behaviour/its outcome
➤ Duration—the length of time a behaviour/situation lasts

Other examples of such units are

➤ Weight
➤ Distance
➤ Cost

When such objective measures are not easy to derive (as with more subjective/complex variables) it is still possible to quantify and measure change by some form of numerical scaling.

2. *Numerical scaling.* This involves assigning numbers to defined levels of the variable under consideration. Each end of the scale is defined as objectively as possible.

Examples

People might be asked to judge pain (substitute anxiety, sadness, activity level, satisfaction etc.) on a scale of 1 to 5 where

1 = no pain
5 = excruciating pain

The measure can be made more sensitive by defining (anchoring) each point on the scale

5 = excruciating pain
4 = a lot of pain
3 = moderate pain
2 = a little pain
1 = no pain

Sometimes anchoring can be in terms of more physical dimensions, for example of behaviour

5 = spat more than twenty times
4 = spat between 10 and twenty times
3 = spat between 5 and 10 times
2 = spat between 1 and 5 times
1 = did not spit at all

The better (and more agreed) is the definition of the points on a scale the more likely such a scale will prove accurate in assessing change.

3. *Goal attainment scaling.* This is a form of numerical scaling applied to specific targets or standards set. It is particularly useful for developing measures of service quality. It organises levels of performance into a hierarchy.

Examples

Contact with family of child in residential school by key worker
1. Unacceptable standard: Telephone calls at less than two weekly intervals
2. Falls below standard: Telephone calls at 8–14 day intervals
3. Minimum standard: One telephone call to family each week
4. Exceeds standard: Telephone contact at 4–6 day intervals

Service user to be taken out to social events by staff each week
1. Unacceptable standard: No off-site evening activity offered during a week
2. Falls below standard: one off-site evening activity offered during a week
3. Minimum standard: two off-site evening activities to be offered during a week
4. Exceeds standard: three or more off-site activities offered during a week

How to Measure

How measures are actually taken of course influences the accuracy of the information and hence the value of performance feedback. Common strategies include

Direct Observation of Behaviour

This is the most accurate way of gathering information—to observe and measure the behaviour or outcome in question. Accuracy is enhanced if

➤ Measurement/recording is carried out as close as possible in time to when the behaviour in question occurs
➤ The observer remains as objective as possible. This is partly a matter of training although it is often helped if the person carrying out the observation is not directly involved in the interaction or event

Video recording can be a very powerful way of directly observing and collecting information for performance feedback. It provides a permanent record which can be analysed repeatedly and at leisure. It is also attractive and motivating for many people in and of itself.

Indirect Measurement of Behaviour

When direct observation is not feasible then information can be gathered indirectly, from others

> face to face

or

> from written records

The accuracy of information gathered in this way is enhanced if

➤ Those whose opinions are sought have themselves been first hand observers of the behaviour or outcome
➤ The information is gathered as soon as possible after the behaviour has occurred
➤ Information is gathered from as many observers as possible
➤ Care is taken to gather information in a way that distinguishes what has actually been observed from the subjective interpretations of a behaviour/situation made by the observer

Self Monitoring

As well as generating information for assessing progress, change itself can be made more likely if the individual (staff or service user) is involved in monitoring her own behaviour. This is because it generates 'on line' performance feedback.

When to Measure

Motivational performance feedback relates

> how things are now

compared to

> how they were at some previous time

Establishing a Baseline Level

A baseline is the current level of performance or a description of the current situation before a new plan is put into action. It is the marker against which subsequent performance and progress can be measured. As for behavioural goals, a statement of baseline performance should state

> *Who* does *what* to *what degree of success*

Examples

Who	Mary
Does what	has attended IPP meetings to observe how they are structured
	has read IPP reports written by other staff
	but

To what degree of success	has never written an IPP report herself
Who	Residents
Does what	visit the local pub once a week
To what degree of success	accompanied by staff
Who	Jo
Does what	is physically aggressive to staff
To what degree of success	on average three times each day

A baseline needs to be established and recorded before any plan is put into action. If this is not done then it is very likely that

> how the situation is now will be forgotten as things start to change

This makes it impossible to judge progress (or otherwise).

A baseline may just be a matter of a single recording (for example of a current level of skill). For more variable factors (for example mood, frequency of a problematic behaviour) then measurement may need to be continued over days or weeks.

A key guideline is that

> measurement should continue until an accurate/stable level has been established

A single measure of a fluctuating factor will not enable an accurate estimate of change to be made. Because it is variable anyway it becomes hard to judge if the present level (an increase or decrease) can be attributed to work put in or might have occurred anyway.

A second important guideline is that

> what is measured and how it is measured should be the same before, during and after action is taken

This is the only way that an accurate judgment about change can be made.

Continuing the Measurement Process

Once a system is established it needs to be sustained. The choice is between

➤ Continuous measurement—the behaviour/activity/situation is recorded each time it occurs
➤ Sample measurement—measurement is taken intermittently (for example, each morning, one day a week, the first time it happens each day, after the plan has been in operation for a week)

Obviously, continuous measurement will be the most accurate, but it will also be the most time consuming. There is no easy answer. It is important to blend

> accuracy

and

> feasibility

This is a judgement call to be made in the light of

➤   What is being monitored
➤   The resources available

Where a sample system is used it is important to try and make sure that information is gathered in a way most likely to be representative of the 'real' situation (as with opinion polls).

Example

A manager was keen to know, monitor and feed back to staff the level of interaction occurring with service users. Rather than relying on her haphazard observations she organised herself to carry out five minute observations when she counted the number and duration of interactions. With careful planning she was able over a period of time to do these observations in each hour of the day and on each day of the week. This gave her a much better overview of the current functioning of her service in this respect.

Where to Record

The information gathered needs to be stored in an organised way if it is going to be possible to analyse change over time. Sometimes this is automatic as with video recording or if the area of concern is the subject of an organisational rule (for example accident/incident records). At other times it will be useful to devise a specific chart to record and store information. Such recording charts will

➤   Act as a memory aid for those who have been charged with recording, reminding them to carry out the recording
➤   Focus those observing/recording on to the areas that have been agreed in advance rather than on to what they may subjectively wish to record
➤   Enhance the quality of information by targeting specific areas and making it easy to record in an abbreviated form

Recording charts should be designed in such a way that information can be entered

➤   Simply
➤   Rapidly
➤   In units of measurement selected in advance

Such charts should state clearly

➤   What is to be recorded
➤   How it is to be recorded

Figures 11.1 and 11.2 provide examples of simple recording charts.

Activity List for Christine

Complete the chart below at the end of each activity

Activity	Tick Activity Completed	Date
Walk		
Cinema		
Swimming		
Shopping		
Dance Class		
Day Trip Out		
Bingo		
Bowling		
Pub		
Snooker		
Fishing		
Painting		
Knitting		
Cooking		
Aromatherapy		
Snoozelen		
TV		

Figure 11.1   A simple chart for recording a client's activities

DELIVERING PERFORMANCE FEEDBACK

Table 11.1 outlines the prerequisites for useful performance feedback.

Table 11.1   Prerequisites for useful performance feedback

Agreement reached between manager and staff on goals and standards
Actions to be done/outcomes to be achieved defined in objective terms
Goals and standards set in measurable terms
Recording procedures prepared
Baseline levels established
Continuing measurement system established

Once these steps have been taken performance and progress can be monitored in a fair and objective way.

The individual/team can now receive feedback on how well actual performance or results compare to the targets set. Knowing that progress has been achieved, goals or standards met will be an important source of positive reinforcement. Recognising any shortfall will

Client's Name: *BOB*
Behaviour to be recorded: *Physical Aggression*

Date	Time	Duration of incident	Description of incident

Figure 11.2   A simple chart for recording a client's behaviour

encourage problem solving. In this sense knowledge of results, whether positive or negative, acts as a 'guidance system' for individuals and teams. However, there are many ways by which performance feedback can be delivered (see below). What they all have in common is that to be maximally effective the method for delivering feedback needs to be

➤ Structured
➤ Specific
➤ Objective

Visually Presented Feedback

Visual feedback has the advantage that

it can be available at all times

Pictures are also

intrinsically attractive to many people

and with careful attention to design and to the use of colour and symbols the motivational impact can be enhanced. Visual formats also

enable the ready integration of information over time

making it easy to see at a glance what has been going on over

days
weeks
months
years

Charts

Graphs and bar charts (see Figures 11.3 and 11.4) can be used to display progress over time in any behaviour or subjective state that has been quantified in numerical units. The effectiveness of such methods can be enhanced by careful planning so that the chart

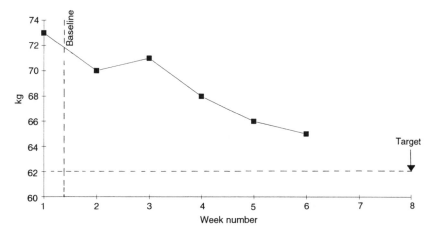

Figure 11.3   A personal weight chart

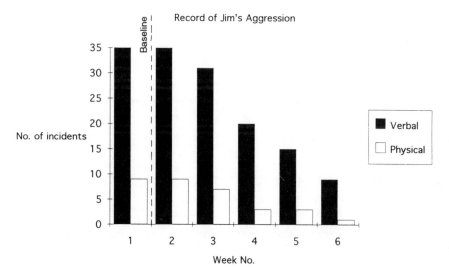

Figure 11.4   A bar chart recording incidents of aggression

> Covers all possible 'scores'
> Can easily incorporate the amount of time over which the variable is being
  monitored
> Shows both the baseline level and the goal envisaged
> Is easy to update

Tick charts (Figure 11.5)—where activities/behaviours are ticked as they occur—are another simple format for generating feedback information. Again careful attention to design will enhance the value and impact of the information.

DRY BEDS

Week No	Mon	Tue	Wed	Thur	Fri	Sat	Sun	Total	Target
1			✓			✓	✓	3	3
2	✓		✓		✓			3	4
3									4
4									
5									
6									
7									
8									

Figure 11.5   A tick chart

Gathering information and completing charts can be done by hand or by computer.

Video Recording

For some areas of work (such as skill development, users or staff) video can be a powerful feedback tool. Consecutive videos, starting with the baseline level, enable judgements to be made about change over time in a format that is extremely 'friendly' to most people. The technology now is also simple to use and delivers high quality pictures under a wide range of conditions.

Verbally Presented Feedback

Giving feedback socially is another way for communicating information about results. This can be done in a number of ways:

> Face to face
> In writing

However it is done a number of important principles need to be observed if the motivational impact is to be maximised. It is vital that the feedback

➤ Is structured
➤ Focusses upon objective performance *not* personal characteristics

> your performance fell short of/exceeded the standard by . . .

not

> you're stupid, lazy, clever, sensitive

Verbal feedback should state

➤ What has actually been done
➤ The previous situation or baseline level
➤ The standard or goal set
➤ The present situation and how it compares with the above

Examples

You last telephoned Ann's parents nine days ago (action taken)
The minimum contact required with parents is one telephone call each week (standard preset)
Your action falls below the minimum level of contact required (comparison of behaviour to standard)
Please ensure that you telephone them today and in future do not allow more than seven days to pass without telephoning them.

The IPP report which you wrote (action taken)
Followed exactly the format that we use here (comparison to standard)
Your grammar and spelling were accurate and needed no correcting (comparison to goal)
The report was ready three days before the deadline date
(comparison to goal)
In future you will not need to have your reports checked by your supervisor.

Verbal feedback can also be provided in writing and this format is often used to record skills and achievements by means of

➤ Testimonials
➤ Certificates of competence
➤ Certificates of achievement

Examples

Ann Smith
Ann has attended the following short courses this year:
The understanding of aggressive and challenging behaviour
Understanding autism
An ordinary life

The management of challenging behaviour

She has subsequently set up assessment procedures to analyse the challenging behaviours of two service users and from these guided the team to developing intervention programmes for both clients. Both programmes led to a reduction of the challenges being presented by the service users.

James Brown
James has achieved a 100% attendance record at work during the last year
He is declared the most healthy member of the staff team!

CONCLUSIONS

Knowledge about the outcome of work efforts makes an important contribution to performance at work. Such results strengthen successful practices and challenge underfunctioning or unsuccessful practices. In addition the presence of systems which emphasise accurate information and the importance of outcomes will help to generate achievement motivations in those who do not bring them automatically to the workplace. Knowledge of results is therefore a vital tool in the battle to generate and to sustain high quality service provision.

SUMMARY

1. KNOWLEDGE OF RESULTS IS AN IMPORTANT SOURCE OF REINFORCEMENT AND PROBLEM SOLVING IN THE WORKPLACE.

2. IF INFORMATION ABOUT WORK PERFORMANCE IS TO BE USEFUL THEN WORK EXPECTATIONS MUST BE DEFINED IN CLEAR AND SPECIFIC TERMS.

3. GOALS AND MINIMUM WORK STANDARDS NEED TO BE STATED IN UNITS WHICH ARE MEASURABLE.

4. BASELINE LEVELS OF PERFORMANCE NEED TO BE ESTABLISHED AND RECORDED SO AS TO PROVIDE A YARDSTICK FOR CHANGE.

5. SIMPLE, OBJECTIVE METHODS ARE NEEDED TO RECORD PERFORMANCE OVER TIME.

6. A SYSTEM FOR GATHERING INFORMATION OVER TIME NEEDS TO BE DECIDED UPON.

7. THE OUTCOME OF WORK EFFORT SHOULD BE FED BACK IN CLEAR AND OBJECTIVE TERMS, RELATING THE PRESENT SITUATION TO BOTH THE BASELINE AND THE GOAL/STANDARD SET.

8. FEEDBACK CAN BE PRESENTED IN BOTH PICTORIAL AND VERBAL FORMATS.

Manager's toolkit	
Tools	Applications
A behavioural vocabulary	Define goals and standards. Measure progress objectively. Provide objective verbal feedback
Goal setting	Establish targets/standards for work performance
Giving feedback (verbal/written)	Reinforce good practices. Challenge poor practices
Observation	Monitor progress
Recording	Monitor progress
Video camera skills	Monitor progress
Computer skills	Monitor progress
Design skills	Develop charts for progress monitoring
Problem solving skills	Design effective monitoring and feedback systems

CHAPTER 12   It's nice to be appreciated

AIMS OF THE CHAPTER

1. TO DISCUSS THE NATURE AND ROLE OF POSITIVE SOCIAL RES-
   ULTS (REINFORCEMENT) IN STRENGTHENING APPROPRIATE
   WORK BEHAVIOUR.

2. TO ANALYSE THE METHODS FOR PROVIDING POSITIVE SOCIAL
   RESULTS SO AS TO GAIN MAXIMUM EFFECT.

3. TO OUTLINE SOME OF THE BLOCKS TO THE FREQUENT USAGE OF
   SOCIAL REINFORCEMENT.

4. TO IDENTIFY WAYS OF MAXIMISING THE OPPORTUNITIES FOR
   AND FREQUENCY OF SOCIAL REINFORCEMENT IN THE
   WORKPLACE.

INTRODUCTION

For many people

   it is how others respond to them

that is an important influence over what they do. The social results that follow a particular action will determine whether that action will be repeated. A positive response from others will encourage many people to repeat/continue the action concerned.

There are a range of positive responses from others that may be influential. People may want to be

➤ Liked
➤ Accepted
➤ Valued
➤ Respected
➤ Admired

Thus social reinforcement can be expressed as

➤ Gratitude
➤ Praise
➤ Valuation
➤ Appreciation

Such social results have a number of common characteristics. They are

➤ Powerful . . . for many people
➤ Readily available
➤ Quick to administer
➤ Less easily tired of . . . compared to other reinforcers

In theory they look the ideal means of strengthening good quality performance at work. In practice they are far too little used

---

Exercise

Record your own behaviour over several days by noting each time that you use positive social reinforcement with staff and each time that you use criticism or correction. Use a simple tick chart, divided into two columns.

Examples of social reinforcement: praise, valuation, acknowledgement of effort, thanks

Examples of criticism: nagging, telling off

Note: the total number of times that you use social reinforcement
the ratio of reinforcement to criticism

There might be many explanations as to why rates of social reinforcement are typically low. This chapter will focus on four 'inhibitors'.

Managers may

➤ Not know how to deliver social reinforcement in general
➤ Not know how to use such results to maximum effect
➤ Not feel comfortable relating to staff in this way

Staff may

➤ Not feel comfortable receiving this kind of attention from managers

KNOWING HOW TO DELIVER SOCIAL REINFORCEMENT

In everyday language social reinforcement is often interpreted as meaning such general statements as

Well done
Thank you
That was great
You're so clever
That was nice

These messages may be pleasant to hear—produce a general 'warm glow'. This is not a bad thing but does not make a clear link between the good feeling and a specific action (see Chapter 11). This opens up grounds for misunderstanding, staff interpreting the reason for comment in a different way to that intended by the manager.

On the other hand such messages may be rejected because the recipient

➤ Finds them condescending
➤ Is embarrassed
➤ Disagrees with the 'personality' assessment ('I'm not clever')

Either way the outcome is less than optimal if the aim is to strengthen specific actions that staff have taken.

For maximum impact social reinforcement, just like performance feedback (Chapter 11), should be as specific as possible. It should leave the recipient in no doubt as to

       what action
and   is being reinforced
       why this action

Included in the 'why' is information about

➤ The emotional impact that the staff's behaviour had on the manager
➤ The relationship of the action to the service mission

These elements distinguish social reinforcement from knowledge of results.

Thus social reinforcement should contain as much as possible of the following information:

➤ The specific staff action being commented upon
➤ Specific positive aspects of the action
➤ The emotional impact of the action on the person reinforcing
➤ The concrete and immediate positive effect of the action
➤ How the action relates to the service mission

Examples

Action performed	The way you handled that irate client was excellent
Specific positive aspects of the action	You looked sympathetic, your voice remained calm, you listened patiently to his complaint
Emotional impact of the action on you	I was very impressed with your 'people' skills
Concrete and immediate positive effect of action	He calmed down quite quickly and was able to sort out the misunderstanding
How action relates to mission	You treated him with respect and dignity throughout

Action performed	Thank you for writing that report so promptly
Specific positive aspects of the action	It was ready three days before the meeting
Emotional impact of the action on you	That was a great relief to me because it avoided unnecessary pressures on me
Concrete and immediate positive effect of action	It meant that the report could be circulated in plenty of time so that everyone had a chance to read it. We were then able to make some practical decisions during the meeting
How action relates to mission	Users will benefit from an improved and more efficient service

In practice it may be difficult to get all the elements together at one go but it is important to work towards this. Knowing how to give social reinforcement is in part knowing what the content should be.

The other main contributors to 'know-how' are the actual delivery skills—the

➤ Language used
➤ Tone of voice
➤ Body language

These are the kinds of performance skills that require behavioural practice rather than verbal description. However, one thing that does need to be stated is that

>   social reinforcement must be sincere

The person reinforcing must believe the message that she is communicating. Without this condition being met the recipient is likely to feel patronised or deceived and the whole exercise will be counterproductive.

However, even with skilled and sincere delivery the impact of social reinforcement will be less than optimal unless attention is given to other conditions.

MAXIMISING THE IMPACT OF SOCIAL REINFORCEMENT

Attention to three additional factors is relevant here.

Credibility

Social reinforcement is just that—it is about

>   person to person interaction and valuing

Thus the quality of the relationship between the participants influences whether or not a particular interaction is regarded as reinforcing. Social reinforcement can only work where a quality relationship between staff and manager exists. This is more to do with respect than liking. Such respect may be based upon a number of manager characteristics:

➤ Formal authority (the power to hire, fire, discipline, reward)
➤ Technical skills (being demonstrably good at the job the service does)
➤ Social skills (being supportive, a good listener, showing respect for others, being honest, reliable)

In terms of empowering social reinforcement

> technical and social respect are more important than respect for formal authority—they have to be earned, they do not come with the role

Building credibility is therefore a vital management task if social reinforcement from the manager is to be a powerful influence over staff behaviour. The bulk of this book is about ways of acting that help to develop CREDIBILITY and INFLUENCE. It is important at this point just to reiterate its centrality in relation to social reinforcement.

The other determinants of reinforcer impact are more technical in nature.

The Timing of Reinforcement

For maximum effect reinforcement should occur

> as closely in time as is possible to the staff action that is being reinforced

An immediate response is ideal. When for practical reasons immediacy is impossible and reinforcement must be delayed, it is important

> to establish a direct link between the action being reinforced and the reinforcer itself by specifying to the individual precisely which behaviour or achievement is being reinforced

The Frequency of Reinforcement

For the technically minded this refers to 'schedules' of reinforcement. For the purpose of this text two important distinctions need to be made

For Promoting New Actions

In the situation where staff are

> putting a new plan into action
> practising new skills
> working to new standards

then positive social results need to be delivered

at a high frequency—as often as is practically possible

Change is always difficult, old ways are always easier to go back to, added incentive is needed if staff are to persevere.

For Maintaining Quality Actions

Good quality work should never be left entirely unremarked, even if it has become almost routine. As new skills or ways of working become consolidated there should be

a gradual reduction in frequency of reinforcement

but not

to zero levels

Maintaining reinforcement should have two qualities

➤ Intermittency—it should occur every so often not continually
➤ Unpredictability—its occurrence should have something of a surprise element (not always at the same time, in the same meeting etc.). This makes it more noticeable and will add to the impact on staff functioning.

FEELING COMFORTABLE GIVING AND RECEIVING SOCIAL REINFORCEMENT

One reason that social reinforcement is underused is that people often feel uncomfortable

giving

and

receiving

it.

Anxiety and embarrassment about giving may stop an individual engaging in the behaviour and practising expressing himself in this way:

➤ Skills are hard to develop without practice
➤ Without practice the discomfort never gets overcome with the result that
➤ Reinforcement occurs at a low level or not at all

This is compounded if there is discomfort receiving. People may feel embarrassed at being praised or thanked (modesty is a value often deeply ingrained from childhood). This may lead them to reject or to downplay the communication:

it was nothing
I was only doing my job
someone had to do it

Such a response may effectively punish the person giving the social reinforcement so that they become less likely to do it in the future. It is another of those negative spirals which leads to a work environment deprived of a powerful source of reinforcement and hence a powerful support to quality.

The problem needs to be tackled from both directions.

Giving

This is tackled in part by practice, taking on the points made earlier about content. If giving social reinforcement is problematic it would be better to focus initially on

➤ People who are likely to respond in a positive way
➤ More structured situations (such as supervision) where what is to be said and how to say it can be planned in advance

Receiving

Receiving reinforcement is as much a skill as giving it. Thus staff may need to learn this skill. Following the format for giving reinforcement, a parallel format indicates that a receiver should

➤ Acknowledge the reinforcement
➤ State its emotional impact

He can also

➤ Expand on the reason for the emotional impact
➤ Relate it back to the action of the sender

Examples

Acknowledge the reinforcement	Thank you for your comment
State its emotional impact	That's nice to hear
Expand on the reason for the emotional impact	I really wasn't sure if I was handling the situation well
Relate it back to the action of the sender	You've given me a bit more confidence now
Acknowledge the reinforcement	I appreciate you saying that
State its emotional impact	That makes me feel good
Expand on the reason for the emotional impact	I worked very hard on that report
Relate it back to the action of the sender	I'm pleased that you noticed

One way of developing both giving and receiving skills is to use formal group exercises.

Giving and Receiving—a Team Building Exercise

In Chapter 7, one of the team building exercises described was Appreciations. This could be adapted to incorporate the giving and receiving formats outlined above. An additional adaptation would be to use groups of three or four instead of pairs so that the exercise can be done with observer(s) who can provide feedback both on the giving and receiving elements.

In this way not only would

> the specific skills involved be enhanced
> the anxieties decreased

but also

> a contribution would be made to general team development

It is also likely that, constructed in this way

> it would raise the likelihood of social reinforcement being used by all members of the team on an informal basis

This makes for a very powerful impact on the functioning of all members of the team, staff and managers alike and this relates to the next area for discussion.

OPPORTUNITIES FOR DELIVERING SOCIAL REINFORCEMENT

Direct Manager–Staff Social Reinforcement

Presence on the 'Shop Floor'

Management is a multifaceted job. Many of its pressures, particularly those related to

> financial resource management
> agency accountability
> general administration

take the manager away from the core work of the service. This means that the manager rarely observes the staff's day to day performance on the job. Staff performance is monitored indirectly—through

> the reports of others

or

> of the staff themselves

This situation makes it hard to use social reinforcement in a maximally effective way. Presence during the work of the service enables the manager to

➤   Observe good practice
➤   Provide social reinforcement close in time to the actions of staff

It is therefore vital to cultivate the practice of what has been called 'management by wandering about'. Time should be

> scheduled and allocated regularly

to working alongside/observing the staff. Such practice not only makes it possible to use social reinforcement in a very influential way, it also

➤   Demonstrates to the team that they and their work are valued
➤   Provides a positive role model for staff in terms of work practices, problem solving and use of social reinforcement
➤   Enables the manager to provide coaching or teaching about specific tasks to specific individuals with immediate feedback about performance

Staff Supervision

Staff supervision in human service tends to be relatively infrequent:

> weekly
> fortnightly
> monthly
> . . . or even longer

Thus social reinforcement for work performance may be far removed in time from that performance. If, in addition, the information available about work performance is indirect (not based on the manager's observations) then the chances of an accurate link between specific actions and reinforcement are further reduced.

Thus to deliver social reinforcement via supervision means that discussion on performance in that context should relate closely to

➤   Agreed goals and standards (see Chapter 11)
➤   Clear and objective measures of outcome and performance which have been established in advance

This permits greater specificity in the feedback and hence increases the power of social reinforcement.

Encouraging the Use of Social Reinforcement Within the Team

Even with time allocated to 'wandering about' a manager cannot be available at all times to provide the level of social reinforcement and evaluation which a team is likely to need in order to sustain high quality performance. As a result

> individuals are likely to be receiving only very occasional reinforcement for their efforts . . .

unless

they are able to provide social reinforcement for each other

Team members are

➤ Able to observe one another's performance and efforts
➤ In the ideal position to provide one another with positive feedback, social reinforcement and evaluation

In order to do this

➤ Team members need to learn the skills of giving and receiving social reinforcement
➤ There needs to be active encouragement to practise these skills

Both mastery and practice are encouraged by

➤ Role modelling—seeing the manager giving and receiving social reinforcement skilfully

This can be done in the course of everyday work (see above). In addition time can be set aside in team meetings for team members to say something positive about other individual team members.

Mastery can be developed by

➤ Adaptation of the Appreciations exercise (see above)

Practice can be encouraged by

➤ Reminders
  – at meetings
  – posted in the workplace
➤ Setting targets for each staff member to deliver a certain amount of social reinforcement on a daily/weekly basis

Public Recognition

There are a number of more formal means of delivering social reinforcement, from a variety of sources, which may be useful for acknowledging special achievement. These include

➤ Writing memos to individuals or the team expressing
  – gratitude for specific work efforts
  – praise for achievements
  – acknowledgement of continuing good quality work
    . . . signed personally of course!
➤ Encouraging senior managers to do the same
➤ Making use of organisational newsletters to acknowledge and show appreciation to individuals or teams for efforts and achievements
➤ Persuading local media to cover the work/achievements of the service

Although removed in time from the work to be acknowledged, such formal and public recognition of achievement or effort has a number of merits.

➤ It provides a permanent record for those concerned about the appreciation of others, providing a 'booster' reinforcement each time reference is made to it
➤ It enhances the power of the reinforcement, because the individual/s concerned are made to feel that their efforts and performance must be exceptional to warrant such public recognition
➤ It enhances the power of the reinforcement because those involved can share the recognition that they have received with family and friends outside of the workplace and thereby know that their work efforts are being recognised beyond the immediate work environment

CONCLUSIONS

Positive social reinforcement is a powerful tool for encouraging and sustaining high quality staff performance. Maximising this potential requires attention to

➤ Technical aspects of reinforcement
➤ Skill aspects in terms of how to deliver and to receive
➤ Cultural aspects in terms of removing blocks which inhibit the use of social reinforcement and creating a climate which sustains its use

Whilst some of the approaches suggested may seem rather crude and culturally alien it is our firm belief that social reinforcement is a simple but much underused tool for helping people in difficult jobs to do good quality work. Such underusage requires urgent attention.

SUMMARY

1. HIGH QUALITY WORK BEHAVIOUR IS BETTER SUSTAINED BY THE USE OF POSITIVE REINFORCEMENT RATHER THAN PUNISHMENT.

2. MANY PEOPLE ARE MOTIVATED AND INFLUENCED BY HOW OTHERS RESPOND TO WHAT THEY DO.

3. SOCIAL VALUATION IS A POWERFUL REINFORCER THAT IS QUICK TO DELIVER AND COSTS NOTHING.

4. FOR MAXIMUM EFFECTIVENESS POSITIVE SOCIAL REINFORCEMENT REQUIRES ATTENTION TO CONTENT, FREQUENCY AND TIMING.

5. THE GIVING OF SOCIAL REINFORCEMENT IS A SKILL WHICH NEEDS TO BE LEARNED AND PRACTISED.

6. THE RECEIVING OF SOCIAL REINFORCEMENT IS A SKILL WHICH NEEDS TO BE LEARNED AND PRACTISED.

7. THOUGHT NEEDS TO BE GIVEN TO CREATING OPPORTUNITIES FOR THE MANAGER TO PROVIDE SOCIAL REINFORCEMENT TO STAFF.

8. THOUGHT NEEDS TO BE GIVEN TO CREATING OPPORTUNITIES AND ENCOURAGEMENT FOR THE STAFF TO PROVIDE SOCIAL REINFORCEMENT TO EACH OTHER.

9. AS WELL AS INFORMAL CHANNELS FOR DELIVERING SOCIAL REINFORCEMENT THERE ARE A RANGE OF FORMAL CHANNELS THAT CAN BE USED TO RECOGNISE SPECIAL ACHIEVEMENTS.

Manager's toolkit	
Tools	Applications
Giving feedback	Deliver positive social reinforcement to staff. Teach skills of giving/receiving social reinforcement
Modelling	Teach and encourage staff to give/receive positive social reinforcement
Time management	Allocate time to 'wandering about'
Observation	Notice opportunities to provide social reinforcement
Persuasion	Elicit social reinforcement for staff from senior managers/ local media
Managing meetings	Create opportunities to teach and practice giving/receiving social reinforcement
Information giving	Explain rationale for and ways of using social reinforcement

CHAPTER 13   ... And it may help if you put your money (or something nice) where your mouth is

AIMS OF THE CHAPTER

1. TO OUTLINE THE ROLE OF MATERIAL REWARDS IN STRENGTH-ENING APPROPRIATE WORK BEHAVIOUR.

2. TO CONSIDER THE VARIOUS TYPES OF MATERIAL REWARDS THAT ARE AVAILABLE TO THE MANAGER.

3. TO ILLUSTRATE WAYS OF USING MATERIAL REWARDS IN ORDER TO ACHIEVE MAXIMUM IMPACT UPON BEHAVIOUR.

INTRODUCTION

This book is about practical ways in which first line managers can

motivate

and

support

staff to work to high standards and thereby deliver a quality service to fellow citizens with long term disabilities. Results are an important focus and two types have already been considered:

➤ Performance feedback
➤ Social valuation

This chapter looks at another type of result that can be influential in terms of both job satisfaction and job performance:

➤ Material results

Material results are those related to consumer goods and services. Money is the most obvious such result. Money itself has little value—it is a token that enables the individual to access goods and services in our society. It becomes valuable because it can be exchanged for items that the individual wants or needs. But behaviour can be influenced by a range of other material results:

➤ Direct rewards such as prizes (food, drink, electrical goods)

➤ Other tokens such as points, stars and tickets that can then be exchanged for goods or services (such as the schemes run by many petrol companies)

It is important to take a broad look at material rewards as the most obvious one—money—may be the very one over which a first line manager has very little control. However, given the importance attached to money it will be considered first.

WAGE STRUCTURES AND BONUS SCHEMES—ORGANISATIONAL REWARDS

From a behavioural perspective any attempt to use material results to influence behaviour can be judged by the criteria outlined in previous chapters.

Positive reinforcement requires a contingency relationship between a behaviour and the reinforcing event—the reinforcing event depends upon the behaviour occurring.

Positive reinforcement is most likely to increase and sustain a behaviour if it occurs close in time to that behaviour.

Positive reinforcement will increase new behaviours if it occurs frequently.

Positive reinforcement will sustain current behaviours if it occurs intermittently and unpredictably.

In addition, schemes that systematise the use of rewards are likely to be judged by social criteria

Satisfaction with a reward scheme will in part be related to its perceived fairness

However, satisfaction with a scheme is not necessarily an indication of how effective the scheme might be in influencing behaviour.

With these criteria in mind organisational reward systems can be considered.

Regular Pay

Wage/salary levels are an important influence upon

➤ Recruitment
➤ Retention
➤ Satisfaction

However, their structure is such as to have little direct influence upon

➤ The quality of work performance

Traditionally

➤ Pay is received at fixed intervals (weekly/monthly)

➤   Its delivery is not dependent directly upon the employee behaving in any particular way
➤   Its delivery is only partly related to even turning up at work

Performance Related Pay

Performance related pay is a more likely way of influencing behaviour as it links re-muneration to designated staff performances. However, even here there are limitations

➤   Only a small part of pay received will be performance related
➤   Only a small number of performances will be linked to pay
➤   The designated performances are likely to be the same for everyone—thus making it hard to tailor the scheme to individual needs
➤   The schemes are usually for individuals whereas some of the key performances in human services will be team efforts
➤   There will be little link in time between pay and performance as remuneration is generally reviewed annually. This means no close link between current or even recent work behaviour and pay

Bonus Schemes

Bonus schemes offer more flexibility in terms of

➤   Timing
➤   Team or individual basis for reward
➤   Frequency

Bonus schemes can involve

➤   Monetary reward
➤   Direct material rewards (such as a holiday break)
    or even
➤   The chance to win material rewards (the bonus is a lottery ticket for a prize draw and the number of tickets is strictly limited)

Whilst bonus schemes have considerable potential for influencing staff behaviour, in practice schemes are

➤   Often inflexible, based upon an organisation-wide policy
➤   Rarely under the control of first line managers

Thus organisational reward schemes related to the remuneration system are

➤   Not particularly useful for influencing specific aspects of staff behaviour
➤   Usually not under the control of first line managers

However, there may be

other types of material reinforcement
other ways of using material reinforcement

that are feasible for first line managers and provide a useful addition to the other types of results that have been discussed in previous chapters (performance feedback and social valuation).

MATERIAL REWARDS POTENTIALLY AVAILABLE TO THE FIRST LINE MANAGER

There are a number of such rewards which are free or may be relatively inexpensive to purchase.

Activities or 'Treats'

Each work setting will offer control over a number of activities which might be used to reinforce specific team or individual actions. Examples might include

- Access to favoured work activities
- Attendance at off site training courses
- Attendance at academic conferences
- Extra time for lunch breaks
- Choice over day off
- Choice over shift pattern
- Manager making tea and providing biscuits for each team meeting for a month
- Lunch/dinner with a senior person in the organisation

Symbolic Rewards

These have little or no material value but gain power because they symbolise achievement and social valuation. Examples might include

- A trophy or cup
- A certificate
- A specially printed t-shirt or sweatshirt
- A special badge or pen
- Lunch/tea in one's honour
- 'Mention in dispatches'—award list published in organisation newsletter/bulletin board
- A commemorative photograph

Consumable Rewards

These are goods which may be obtained at small expense. It would be useful to engage senior management in discussions to allocate a small budget for this purpose. Examples might include

➤ Chocolates/sweets
➤ Bottle of wine/champagne
➤ Flowers/pot plant
➤ Basket of fruit
➤ Toiletries
➤ Gift token

Secondary Rewards

These are items which are not valuable in themselves but are the means for getting access to the other rewards outlined above. Examples might include

➤ Points
➤ Tokens
➤ Stars
➤ Prize draw tickets

When considering use of material rewards two additional considerations need to be borne in mind, over and above the criteria mentioned earlier.

> **Reinforcers are individually based—what one person finds reinforcing is a matter of indifference to another.**

> **Over-frequent usage of a particular reward can lead to satiation and boredom and consequent loss of reinforcing potential of that item/activity.**

What is available in terms of reinforcers depends upon

➤ The work setting
➤ The imagination of the manager

With this in mind Figure 13.1 offers an exercise to stimulate thinking about the material rewards potentially available in the reader's own workplace.

WAYS OF USING MATERIAL REINFORCEMENT TO INFLUENCE WORK FUNCTIONING

Activity Sequencing

A simple but effective way of increasing the likelihood that

> dull
> routine
> difficult
> unpleasant

activities will get done is to link their completion to a more interesting task or activity. This requires careful planning of daily activities.

Exercise

Under the heading below make a list of potential reinforcers that you might place at your disposal or which you could make available within your work setting which would be under your individual control.

Activities within workplace

Activities outside of workplace

Material Rewards

Symbolic Rewards or Prizes

Figure 13.1 Potential reinforcers exercise

Examples

First clean the bathroom
Then take Frank shopping

First write the reports
Then take Andrew and Sarah bowling

With inefficient activity planning staff will start with interesting/pleasant activities. Knowledge that completion of these activities will mean that the unpleasant chores will have to be done is likely to slow down their completion so that either no time is left or only a very small amount of time remains for the dull or difficult tasks . . . and if these are important . . .

With good planning dull or difficult chores will be set first. Access to a more pleasant activity will act as

➤   A direct incentive to complete the tasks

Participation in the more pleasant activity will be

➤   A direct reward for completion of the less pleasant activity

Using Material Rewards to Increase the Strength of Social Reinforcement

The sorts of social reinforcement discussed in Chapter 12 can be made even more powerful by the addition of small material rewards such as

➤   Cakes
➤   Chocolates
➤   A bottle of wine
➤   Flowers
➤   Potted plants

These have little material value in themselves. However, these items are linked socially and culturally to such messages as

> 'thank you'
> 'well done'
> 'let's celebrate'

and can therefore enhance the effect of social reinforcement

Example

Performance feedback	You've all made a special effort these last few months to extend the range of activities outside the home for all the residents. The residents seem happier, there are fewer instances of aggression or temper, and I've noticed that there is a lot more social interaction between the residents.
Social reinforcement	Well done everybody. You've worked really hard and it has clearly paid off.
Material reinforcement	As a way of showing my appreciation I've bought this box of chocolates for you all to share. I hope no-one's on a diet!

Using material rewards in this way should be done intermittently and irregularly in order to

➤   Inject an element of surprise
➤   Avoid satiation—maintain the power of the reinforcement

Incentive Schemes

This is a formal and structured way of using positive material reinforcement for increasing or sustaining particular staff actions. It is a contractual agreement between manager and staff which states

➤   The standard or goal to be achieved
➤   The reward to be earned for its achievement
➤   The time span over which the scheme operates

Setting up such a scheme involves a number of steps, summarised in Table 13.1.

Table 13.1   Summary of steps to establish an incentive scheme

1.   Determine the goal/standard/outcome which is to be reinforced
2.   Decide on whether scheme to involve competition or cooperation between staff
3.   Select reinforcers and methods of use
4.   Establish method of evaluating performance
5.   Establish the criterion for attaining reward
6.   Set dates for review of performance relative to goal/standard and for administration of rewards
7.   Establish method of monitoring and recording performance
8.   Plan the 'awards' ceremony
9.   Plan developments to keep the scheme moving forward

1.   Determine the Goal/Standard/Outcome Which is to be Reinforced

Incentive schemes can be introduced in relation to any area of staff performance. However, given the time and effort required to set up and run such a scheme their most useful application is likely to be in areas where

there are greatest motivational and performance problems amongst the staff team

Whichever the area of work targeted it is important that

the performance/goal/standard is clearly specified (see Chapters 5 and 11)

Examples

Key worker files kept up to date and well organised—correspondence, background information, written guidelines and programmes, recording charts, summaries of progress.

Staff to arrive on time for work and for meetings.

2.   Competition or Cooperation?

Where staff are dependent upon each other for

completion of tasks
attainment of targets

then setting up incentive schemes which encourage competition and individual achievements rather than team effort will be destructive. However, where

there is little interdependence
achievement is solely down to individual effort

then competition can be usefully encouraged.

Examples

Scheme	Key workers to be rewarded for key client learning new skills
Outcome	Competition (inappropriate)—key workers focus exclusively on own clients and neglect teaching other clients.
Scheme	Team reward when any client learns new skill
Outcome	Cooperation (appropriate)—team works together on consistent learning approach with all clients.
Scheme	Key worker with best kept client file to be rewarded.
Outcome	Competition (appropriate)—key workers take care of own files

3.   Select Reinforcers and Methods of Use

Incentive schemes will operate over lengthy time spans. Time elements need to be planned as well as the actual reinforcers that will be used.

Frequency of reinforcement. The greater the problem, the more frequently it occurs, the more frequently the reinforcer will need to be awarded. This of course needs to be balanced against practicalities such as the time available to

➤   Manage the incentive system
➤   Deliver the awards with adequate pomp and ceremony

Types of reinforcers. These should be the most powerful/sought after items that the manager has control over. They will be used infrequently but the system can be set so that staff earn regular 'credits' which count towards the major prize or award. Less sought after and powerful reinforcers can be used more frequently but should be varied in order to

➤   Retain their reinforcing potential
➤   Avoid satiation

Examples

Problem	Punctuality
Severity	Chronic and daily
Reinforcement frequency	Monthly
Reinforcement	Small box of chocolates plus credit towards the annual award of a trophy for the most punctual member of staff

Problem	Key worker files out of date
Severity	New pieces of information come at an approximate rate of one item every two to three weeks. Files can become seriously out of date within three months
Reinforcement frequency	For up to date files—three monthly
Reinforcement	Small posy of flowers plus thank you card written by/on behalf of the client

4. Establish Method of Evaluating Performance

The scheme must specify the method by which performance will be evaluated and this should be as objective as possible.

Examples

Subjective:	vote by secret ballot of all staff . . . to select . . . most helpful team member most good natured team member most hard working team member
Subjective:	assessment by manager . . . to select . . . most up to date and best organised files most innovative work with client
Objective:	the number of times each staff member arrives late for work

5. Establish the Criterion for Attaining Reward

This states

> what . . . has to be done . . . by whom

in order to achieve a reward. This may be

➤ Everyone who achieves the pre-established target
➤ The one/two/three people judged to have produced the best performance

6. Set Dates for Review of Performance Relative to Goal/Standard and for Administration of Rewards

The dates should be established in advance so that the deadlines and/or assessment period are understood by all concerned.

7. Establish Method of Monitoring and Recording Performance

If a system of credits is being used or if performance is being monitored over a lengthy period of time then a visible system of monitoring progress should be used (see Chapter 11).

Colourful and humorous charts can inject

> life
> reminders
> extra incentive

into the system.

8. Plan the 'Awards' Ceremony

The actual awarding may be as important as or more important than the prize itself. Thus the 'ceremony' needs to be planned so that

➤ The significance of the achievement is stressed
➤ Clear performance and social feedback accompanies the material reward
➤ Good fun is had by all

9. Plan Developments to Keep the Scheme Moving Forward

Once started, incentive schemes should not be allowed to

> end by default
> drift into obscurity

They should either be

> formally terminated

or

> developed and adapted according to staff progress and perceived needs

Development might be in terms of

➤ Making targets more difficult
➤ Extending the time span over which performance has to be sustained
➤ Setting new goals/standards

See Figures 13.2 and 13.3 for examples of simple incentive schemes.

Incentive Scheme

Scheme encourages Individual performance. Competitive

The target behaviour: Punctual attendance at all meetings: Includes shift meeting, whole staff meeting, supervision.

Reinforcement:
(i) Small monthly award to person/s with highest punctuality score. This will be a surprise gift which will be varied from month to month.
(ii) Credit towards 'most reliable person of the year' award. This will be a certificate presented at lunch given in the person's honour

Recording : Shift leaders to keep 'late' register for shift meetings
Manager to keep 'late' register for staff meetings
Shift leaders and managers to keep 'late' register for supervision meetings

Display Chart to be revised monthly showing each person's 'lateness' record and credits received. Chart displayed on staff room wall

Dates of Awards: Month runs from first to last day of month.
Monthly award given at first staff meeting of the month.

Annual award given at last staff meeting before Christmas

Most Reliable Person of the Year Award

Given to person with greatest total number of credits earned from

Punctuality scheme
Staff attendance scheme

Figure 13.2 Competitive incentive scheme

CONCLUSIONS

Whilst first line managers have little control over formal organisational reward systems there is scope in other ways for use of material and symbolic reinforcers in a way likely to influence staff functioning. This may be done informally to reward particular effort and achievement or through more formal incentive systems to target key areas of functioning relevant for all staff. It is another tool and again one that is relatively underused in care services.

Incentive Scheme

Scheme - Cooperative

The target outcome: All residents to feed themselves independently, but not necessarily cutting up own food

Reinforcement: Manager and senior manager will cook lunch for all staff.

Recording: Manager to observe residents over meal times at least once a month to assess. To feed back observational assessment monthly to staff team

Date of Reinforcement : Within two weeks of last resident eating independently.

Figure 13.3 Cooperative incentive scheme

SUMMARY

1. ORGANISATIONAL REWARD SYSTEMS SUCH AS PAY STRUCTURES ARE RELATIVELY INFLEXIBLE IN TERMS OF INFLUENCING SPECIFIC INDIVIDUAL STAFF OR TEAM ACTIONS. THEY ARE USUALLY NOT UNDER THE CONTROL OF FIRST LINE MANAGERS.

2. THERE ARE MATERIAL REWARDS AVAILABLE TO MANAGERS AND THESE VARY ACROSS SETTINGS. THEY INCLUDE ACTIVITIES AND PRIVILEGES, SYMBOLIC REWARDS AND MATERIAL REWARDS.

3. MATERIAL REWARDS CAN BE USED BY MANAGERS TO STRENGTHEN THE POWER OF PERFORMANCE FEEDBACK AND SOCIAL REINFORCEMENT.

4. MATERIAL REWARDS CAN BE USED AS A DIRECT INCENTIVE AND REWARD FOR QUALITY WORK PERFORMANCE.

5. FAVOURED ACTIVITIES CAN BE USED AS A REWARD FOR COMPLETION OF LESS FAVOURED ACTIVITIES. THIS REQUIRES PLANNING ON THE PART OF THE MANAGER.

6. MATERIAL REWARDS CAN BE USED INFORMALLY TO SUPPLEMENT SOCIAL VALUATION AND PERFORMANCE FEEDBACK FOR SPECIFIC INDIVIDUAL/TEAM EFFORTS AND ACHIEVEMENT.

7. INCENTIVE AND REWARD SCHEMES CAN BE ESTABLISHED ON A CONTRACTUAL BASIS TO TARGET STAFF ACTIONS WHICH

HAVE PARTICULAR VALUE/PRIORITY IN THE INDIVIDUAL
WORKPLACE.

8. INCENTIVE SCHEMES NEED TO BE PLANNED AND ACTIVELY
MANAGED.

9. INCENTIVE SCHEMES MAY BE SHORT OR LONG TERM.

10. ANY USE OF MATERIAL REINFORCEMENT IS A SUPPLEMENT
NOT AN ALTERNATIVE TO PERFORMANCE FEEDBACK AND SO-
CIAL VALUATION.

Manager's toolkit	
Tools	Applications
Time management	Use of activities as rewards
Planning/problem solving	Set up incentive scheme
Feedback	Deliver material reinforcers skilfully
Persuasion	Extract resources from senior management to support use of material reinforcers
Financial management	Allocate resources available for material reinforcers to achieve maximum impact on performance

CHAPTER 14 No-one can get it right all of the time

AIMS OF THE CHAPTER

1. TO IDENTIFY THE ROLE OF NEGATIVE FEEDBACK (CON-STRUCTIVE CRITICISM) IN THE MANAGEMENT PROCESS.

2. TO IDENTIFY THE PRECONDITIONS FOR MAKING NEGATIVE FEEDBACK AN EFFECTIVE INFLUENCE ON STAFF MOTIVATION AND BEHAVIOUR.

3. TO IDENTIFY HOW IN PRACTICE TO GIVE SUCH FEEDBACK EFFECTIVELY.

4. TO IDENTIFY SOME OF THE COMMON PITFALLS THAT UNDER-MINE THE VALUE OF NEGATIVE FEEDBACK.

INTRODUCTION

This chapter looks at how to respond to staff behaviours towards service users that are

➤ *Unacceptable*—for example shouting, speaking disrespectfully, ignoring that is not part of a planned programme
➤ *Unskilled*—for example lifting, assisting feeding, giving positive reinforcement, prompting . . . in clumsy/ineffective ways

Whilst the emphasis is upon behaviour towards service users the same considerations would apply to behaviour towards colleagues, managers, relatives etc.

It is important that

➤ Unacceptable and unskilled behaviours be reduced
➤ Staff gain the motivation and knowledge to behave in more constructive ways

One way of doing this is to add in results to such behaviours that will achieve these aims. The focus of this chapter is how to deliver negative feedback in ways that will

➤ Decrease the likelihood of unwanted behaviours
➤ Increase the likelihood of positive alternatives

One school of thought suggests that negative feedback should never be used—the focus should be entirely upon positive feedback for positive behaviours. Whilst this raises an interesting philosophical discussion there is a serious practical problem in negative behaviours going unremarked. This is that the negative behaviours may be strengthened by

> ➤ Repetition—the more they are done the more they are likely to be done ('habit')
> ➤ Reward—the behaviours themselves may achieve positive results for the staff which if not checked will strengthen the behaviours

Example

Shouting at someone often achieves immediate relief from pent up feelings of anger and frustration . . . feelings of guilt and embarrassment follow at a later stage and often have less influence over future behaviour under similar circumstances.

Thus it is an important part of the managerial process to respond effectively to occurrences of unskilled or unacceptable staff behaviours. It can serve both to reduce these behaviours and to promote positive alternatives. It is, however, only likely to do so if certain preconditions are met and if the actual process is carried out in a skilful way.

PRECONDITIONS FOR MAKING NEGATIVE FEEDBACK EFFECTIVE

Clear and Agreed Standards

For behaviour to be judged unacceptable or unskilled there need to be

clear and shared standards

against which to judge a specific action. This relates to the content areas of Chapters 3, 5, 7, 10 and 11.

Visible Management

Detecting unacceptable or unskilled practices requires

observation

of the service at work, of the interactions between providers and users. Management from the office, by meetings and memos, will not lead to effective feedback (positive or negative). Management by wandering about will (see Chapter 12).

Positive Context

Negative feedback is less effective if it is the only feedback that staff receive. Exclusive use of negative feedback leads to a range of possible outcomes.

Habituation. People get used to hearing criticism and become less and less affected by it ('water off a duck's back').

Withdrawal. Staff get to feel that they cannot do anything right and start to do the minimum necessary, particularly avoiding showing any initiative (which usually involves a degree of risk taking).

Perseveration. Staff come to see themselves as useless and incompetent and start to live up to this 'role' in relation to the manager by continuing to behave in ways that will attract criticism.

Resentment. A build up of anger may spill over into relationships between staff themselves, between staff and users, between staff and management.

Modelling. If staff receive only negative feedback from status figures then it is quite likely that the 'negative focus' will come to dominate their relationships with service users. For negative feedback to be a useful tool it needs to occur

> In a generally positive context
> Relatively infrequently

Positive feedback should far outweigh negative feedback if the impact of the latter is going to be constructive. As a rule of thumb

> **staff should receive three times more positive than negative feedback.**

Target the Actions not the Person

The focus of the negative feedback should always be on

> something specific that the staff member did or did not do

It should not be put in terms of general negative characteristics attributed to the staff member.

Examples

There is a difference between saying to a staff member:

'You're a bully' *and* 'I did not like the fact that you shouted at Fred just now'

'You're lazy' *and* 'The clients had nothing meaningful to engage them'

'You're stupid' *and* 'Let me show you a better way to help Maisie understand what you wanted her to do'

If the feedback focuses upon general characteristics

> It is felt as very threatening by the receiver

➤ The anger and resentment generated may well lead to rejection of the feedback
➤ The anger and resentment may precipitate a full scale row in which the main point of the feedback will be lost
➤ It is wide open to challenge

Examples

'I'm not a bully, I spent hours with Fred this morning helping him to dress himself'

'I'm not lazy, I had just spent the whole afternoon taking a group out and I would remind you that I have been coming in my own time to staff training sessions'

➤ It leaves the staff member no way out

Personal characteristics are generally thought to be unchangeable. Giving someone such characteristics gives no indication of the specific changes needed and opens up the possibility of the self fulfilling prophecy—people have a habit of living up to the labels given to them (. . . 'you think that was lazy, just wait and see what really being lazy is!').

Thus negative feedback will only be effective if it deals with

specific staff behaviours that have been observed

and

about which there can be little argument as to their occurrence

The Procedure Should Always Incorporate Information on What Would Have Been a Better Way to Act

Suppressing or decreasing a behaviour does not necessarily leave the individual any the wiser as to what would have been the appropriate ways to behave in the situation. Therefore it is important that the staff member comes away from the interaction knowing

➤ Exactly what he did that was problematic
➤ Exactly how he could have acted differently in the situation

The Procedure Should Avoid Linking Behaviour to Sanctions

In principle decreasing behaviour is more reliably effected if a significant cost to the individual follows quickly after the behaviour. But this principle has a number of pitfalls in the practice of care services that makes its use in the present context undesirable.

➤ There are few sanctions actually available to a manager
➤ Those that are available will usually only come into force long after the specific incident has occurred, thus reducing the likelihood of the sanction having any impact on behaviour

➤ Those that are available will usually be linked to formal disciplinary procedures

Formal disciplinary procedures need to be very clearly separated from the day to day business of interacting and giving feedback. Some instances of unacceptable or unskilled behaviours will be grounds for formal disciplining. Most will not. Formal disciplinary procedures are guided by rules primarily related to employment law rather than behaviour change.

In these circumstances raising the issue of sanctions is likely to mean

➤ Making threats which cannot be fulfilled. There is no effect on behaviour and a loss of credibility for the manager
➤ Raising arguments about rights. This will distract from the main point of the interaction

Thus giving negative feedback in the everyday management process is better effected by avoiding the incorporation of sanctions and threats.

GIVING NEGATIVE FEEDBACK—SPECIFIC PRACTICE GUIDELINES

The basic elements (summarised in Table 14.1) are

Know the Facts

The grounds for feedback must be

some specific action that a staff member has taken or failed to take

This means that the staff member concerned must have been observed—preferably by the manager herself or by a witness giving a clear account. If the facts are not clear then they need to be established before any feedback is given. Assumptions must never be made.

Table 14.1 Key elements in giving negative feedback

Know the facts
Be clear about what is to be achieved by the feedback
Act swiftly
Find a private area
First ask
Then tell–show
Do not be sidetracked
Get the staff member to summarise
Close

Be Clear About What is to be Achieved by the Feedback

It is important that the person giving the feedback is very clear about the outcome that he is trying to achieve by the feedback process. It is important to have to the forefront which staff behaviours need to be changed:

> Which to decrease
> Which to increase

It is all too easy for negative feedback to divert into a blazing row or a cosy chat. It may be diverted because of

> The emotional state of the person giving the feedback (anger at what has happened, anxiety about confronting staff)
> The quality of the overall relationship between the manager and the staff member (working out dislikes, fearful of damaging a positive relationship)

These effects become less likely if the person giving the feedback consciously brings to mind its purposes.

Act Swiftly

The closer in time the feedback is to the actual staff behaviour of concern the more effective it is likely to be.

Find a Private Area

Giving feedback in public will raise the anxiety of all concerned. It adds extra dimensions of

> Humiliation for the receiver
> Public performance for the giver

Any excessive levels of emotion will

> Disrupt the feedback process by impairing the handling of information
> Create setting conditions for other behaviours (fight—become aggressive; flight—seek to terminate the interaction as quickly as possible, by any means available)

First Ask

Give the staff member the opportunity to state what they think the specific concern is. If this is identified correctly, question to elicit

> Why this is a concern
> What would have been a more appropriate way to act in the situation

Asking demonstrates respect and enhances commitment to the solution.

Lecturing about something that the individual already knows will not enhance the impact of the feedback.

Then Tell–Show

State clearly

> The actions identified as inappropriate
> The alternative actions that would have been more satisfactory in the situation

Always use 'I' statements to indicate this is an important matter for you personally—you are not acting on other people's behalf.

If possible, model the alternative actions and get the staff member to demonstrate these. Give reasons for what is being said by linking the specific actions concerned (positive and negative) to core service values.

Back the verbal interaction with appropriate non-verbal behaviour—firm tone of voice, eye contact, serious facial expression.

Do Not be Sidetracked

The staff member may bring up other issues of concern, usually as some form of explanation and justification for what happened. These should not be dealt with as part of the feedback interaction. A separate occasion should be organised to discuss with the staff member these other issues. Likewise the person giving the feedback should not bring other issues into the interaction ('. . . and another thing, while we're on the subject', which 'we' usually were not).

Get the Staff Member to Summarise

The staff member should be asked to summarise the interaction and identify

> The specific actions to be avoided
> The positive alternatives to be practised
> The reasons for all this in relation to the overall purpose of the service

If a further discussion is needed to follow up these issues or to deal with other issues raised it should be made at this point.

Close

End the interaction.

Such feedback interactions should be brief, serious and focussed. The whole process should last no more than a few minutes.

COMMON PITFALLS IN GIVING FEEDBACK

The power of negative feedback can be undermined in a number of ways (summarised in Table 14.2).

Table 14.2   Summary of common pitfalls in giving negative feedback

Delay
Turning a specific individual concern into a group criticism
Inappropriate arousal induction
Using the interaction to achieve other purposes
Clouding
Behaving bizarrely

Delay

Sometimes sheer practicalities make it difficult to give negative feedback soon after the event. However, giving feedback is not easy and can be put off in order to avoid the anxiety evoked by confronting directly staff behaviour. The longer the delay, the less effective the result in terms of changes in staff behaviour and motivation.

Turning a Specific Individual Concern into a Group Criticism

Because one person is late a general memo goes round about time keeping. Because one person shouted at a service user in a non-emergency situation there is a five minute lecture in a staff meeting about shouting. This is the worst of all possible interventions

➤ All the staff members who have not behaved in this way may feel insulted
➤ The staff member who did behave in this way may not realise that the point is directed at him

Inappropriate Arousal Induction

Giving feedback is a serious matter—it is not trivial but nor is it the end of the world. It is important to aim for a moderate level of arousal in the recipient—not too much, not too little. It is all too easy to

➤ Trivialise the matter
  – laughing about it
  – talking about lots of more comfortable subjects
  – avoiding eye contact
  – indicating that it is not you but someone else who sees the staff actions as a problem
➤ Escalate the issue
  – shouting

- pointing
- bringing up other things that the staff member has done wrong in the past

Either extreme will render the feedback ineffective—the information will not get through, unhelpful behaviours will be triggered.

Using the Interaction to Achieve Other Purposes

Linked to creating extreme arousal levels, a feedback interaction can sometimes be used to achieve other purposes for the manager.

Retribution. It may be felt that the staff member has acted in an unfair way and should be made to pay for this.

Anger release. A manager may be in an angry state either because of what the staff member has done or for quite other reasons. The feedback interaction may be used to get rid of these uncomfortable feelings.

Thus the outcomes sought are for the manager not the staff member. The interaction will be punitive and abusive. There will be no constructive outcomes in terms of staff behaviour and motivation.

Clouding

Feedback interaction needs to be sharply focused if it is to achieve effects. The likelihood that the core message gets through will be reduced by

➤ Introducing a wide range of other topics to the interaction
➤ Talking in generalities—about behaviour in general, what people in general think

Such clouding may reflect

> personal style ('born to chat')

or, more commonly,

> an attempt by the person giving the feedback to manage his own anxiety about direct confrontation of an issue

The staff member will end up none the wiser about his own actions at the end of such an interchange.

Behaving Bizarrely

Detailed behaviours of the person giving the feedback may distract from or obscure the main messages to be conveyed. Talking about something important whilst

> avoiding eye contact and mumbling

leaping up and down making jokes

gives rather mixed messages (how important is this?). Habits such as

cracking knuckles
fiddling with keys
chewing nails

will act as distractions. Some of these behaviours reflect personal habits or styles, others reflect attempts to manage anxiety. Either way the person giving feedback needs to

become aware of these personal behaviours
control or change them

so that the key purposes of an interaction do not get subverted.

CONCLUSIONS

Giving negative feedback has a limited but useful place in changing staff motivation and behaviour. It is one of the 'results' over which a manager has some control. It should be clearly distinguished from formal disciplinary procedures. It is only likely to be effective if a manager has extensive observational contact with staff and if there is extensive use already being made of positive feedback. The focus is on specific actions of the staff— what was inappropriate and what would have been more appropriate—and how these relate to the overall purpose of the service. The feedback interaction itself needs to be brief and to the point and requires great skill from the person giving the feedback. If all these conditions are met, then giving negative feedback is a useful addition to the manager's means of influencing staff functioning.

SUMMARY

1. UNACCEPTABLE OR UNSKILLED ACTIONS BY STAFF NEED TO BE PICKED UP AND CORRECTED QUICKLY IF THEY ARE NOT TO BECOME ESTABLISHED BEHAVIOUR PATTERNS.

2. PRECONDITIONS FOR EFFECTIVE CORRECTION ARE CLEAR WITH AGREED STANDARDS, EXTENSIVE OBSERVATIONAL CONTACT WITH STAFF AND A CLIMATE IN WHICH POSITIVE FEEDBACK OCCURS FAR MORE FREQUENTLY THAN NEGATIVE FEEDBACK.

3. NEGATIVE FEEDBACK SHOULD FOCUS ON SPECIFIC STAFF ACTIONS NOT PERSONAL CHARACTERISTICS.

4. CORRECTION MUST INCORPORATE INFORMATION ON WHAT WOULD HAVE BEEN THE APPROPRIATE WAY FOR THE STAFF MEMBER TO ACT IN THE SITUATION.

5. GIVING NEGATIVE FEEDBACK SHOULD BE CLEARLY DISTINGUISHED FROM FORMAL DISCIPLINARY PROCEDURES.

6. In order to give negative feedback effectively it is important to know the facts, to know exactly what is to be achieved by the process and to communicate clearly to the staff member.

7. Correction should be given close in time to the occurrence of concern and be done in private.

8. Negative feedback should be brief and to the point.

9. There are a number of common pitfalls which can arise in the feedback process and should be avoided.

Manager's toolkit	
Tools	Applications
Observation	Detect inappropriate staff practices
Giving positive feedback	Encourage appropriate staff practice
Modelling	Encourage appropriate staff practice
Giving negative feedback	Discourage inappropriate staff practice
Formal disciplinary procedures	Discourage inappropriate staff practice. Terminate staff employment
Questioning	Gain information on practice. Elicit insight/problem solving by staff. Show respect for staff
Stating	Give staff information on appropriate/inappropriate actions
Explaining	Link information on actions to broader service purposes. Show respect for staff
Self management of emotional state	Maintain moderate level of arousal to facilitate feedback process
Self control of personal habits	Avoid distraction from main message in communication

SECTION IV   (Di)stress at Work

Thus far the text has focussed upon management action that creates, strengthens and sustains positive motivations for work; and that facilitates positive functioning on a day to day basis. The present section (Chapters 15 and 16) looks at the nature of stress and how this can undermine both job satisfaction and job performance.

There are many pressures that arise in caring for people with long term disabilities whose needs may be hard to understand and hard to meet. The work itself will have difficult and frankly unpleasant elements—for example caring for someone who is dying, dealing with people who are aggressive, managing incontinence. Pressures are increased by the limitations on resources—low staff ratios, lack of space, lack of training. Often also staff lack control over many of the factors which contribute to quality of service—for example the degrading and impersonal environments in which many disabled people spend their lives. These pressures are over and above the inherent complexity of the work itself. The cumulation of these factors can lead to distress and burn out. These will be marked by physical and emotional withdrawal from the work, or by anger, conflict and confrontation.

Thus once the level of stress passes a certain point it becomes a setting condition for poor quality of service. It undermines the positive motivations emphasised in this book. It generates alternative motivations—essentially fight/flight motivations—which are incompatible with sustained relationship oriented work of any quality.

It is important therefore that positive action is taken to

1. Reduce the likelihood of distress occurring in the first place.
2. Recognise early signs of distress so that strategies can be developed to prevent its escalation and to reduce its current level.
3. Provide support for caregivers whose physical and psychological well being has been impaired by the level of stress experienced.

This section therefore analyses the nature of stress and looks at the steps that can be taken at work to prevent or manage constructively its negative effects.

CHAPTER 15 Understanding stress at work

AIMS OF THE CHAPTER

1. TO PRESENT A MODEL FOR UNDERSTANDING STRESS.

2. TO CONSIDER THE NATURE OF WORKPLACE STRESSORS.

3. TO LOOK AT THE COPING PROCESS AND THE RESOURCES THAT PEOPLE HAVE AVAILABLE FOR DEALING WITH THE STRESSORS ENCOUNTERED.

4. TO CONSIDER THE EFFECTS OF COPING WITH STRESSORS.

5. TO IDENTIFY THE SIGNS OF DISTRESS AND BURN OUT.

INTRODUCTION

The term stress is often associated with something bad. In popular terms stress is equated with anxiety or tension. Sometimes it is referred to as an illness. Stress is none of these things.

Stress is *not*

➤   Anxiety
➤   Nervous tension
➤   An illness

Stress is what people experience when they find

➤   A mismatch between
    –   their perception of a particular situation and
    –   their belief about how that situation ought to be
➤   A mismatch between
    –   a perceived state, and
    –   a desired state

The mismatch is

➤   In a negative direction
➤   Deemed important by the individual

Examples

Perceived state	Desired state
I'm not on course for meeting the deadline	To meet the deadline
I thought my performance was average	To do better than average
This person is getting very upset	For the person to calm

This definition of stress shows that it is part of everyday life. Negative mismatches between perceived and desired states occur continually, at home and at work. If they did not, life would present no challenges, it would be dull and predictable.

Stress is therefore

not only

      unavoidable

but also

      highly desirable

The right level of stress will enhance performance because the individual focusses attention and channels energy into redressing the imbalance between the perceived and the desired state (for example, works harder to meet the deadline). In so far as the effort is successful the individual may experience positive feelings and grow in self confidence/self esteem. At the very least a sense of relief will be felt.

Negative effects occur only when

➤ The mismatch is too great (I can't do it)
➤ The mismatch goes on for too long (I can't take much more, I'm exhausted)
➤ There are too many mismatches at one time (I don't know where to start)
➤ The resolution requires unpleasant methods (I hate doing this)

That is, when the problems faced exceed the capacity to cope. Coping abilities themselves vary and depend upon a number of factors. It is important to understand these factors if appropriate action is to be taken by managers to

➤ Reduce the likelihood of adverse effects upon individual staff members
➤ Help those staff members who experience difficulties following their efforts to cope with stressors

A MODEL OF STRESS AND COPING

Figure 15.1 illustrates a model of stress and coping. It is a flow diagram depicting the various factors that influence

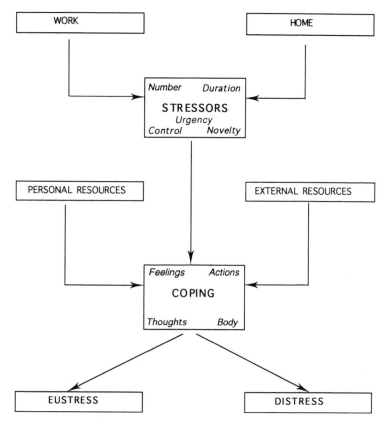

Figure 15.1 A model of stress and coping

➤ The stress experienced
➤ The effectiveness of coping

The model has a number of elements:

Stressors

These are the factors that create a mismatch between how a situation is perceived and how the individual would like it to be. Stressors are events or situations occurring at work or within one's personal life. They can be

➤ Major events—such as redundancy, promotion, divorce or bereavement
➤ Minor events—such as unexpected visitors, extra work to complete, an argument
➤ Ongoing concerns—such as worry about aging, worry about family members, worry about career direction

Stressors are often associated with

➤ Uncertainty
➤ Threat

➤ Conflict
➤ Frustration
➤ Competitiveness
➤ Loss
➤ Change
➤ Unpleasantness

Work Related Stressors

Many stressors at work are the reverse of the conditions which have been described in this book as important for creating and sustaining staff motivation. These factors involve problems in

➤ Job content
  – degree of difficulty
  – dangerousness/unpleasantness
  – volume
  – number of things interfering with getting the job done
➤ Role factors
  – clarity of role
  – conflict between the various roles an individual holds
  – conflicting expectations from others about an individual's role
  – suitability of role to the way the individual perceives her status
➤ Power distribution
  – level of personal control over decision making/way the job is done
➤ Social relationships
  – degree of harmony/conflict
  – availability of support from managers, colleagues, staff
➤ Physical environment
  – space, noise, light, temperature, smell, air quality
➤ Development opportunities
  – for learning and personal growth
  – for career development
➤ Organisational change
  – job security
  – new tasks/roles

Personal Life Stressors

Stressors can arise in many areas including

➤ Personal relationships
  – loss
  – conflict
  – lack of satisfaction
➤ Traumatic events

- – accidents
- – crimes
- – abusive experiences
➤ Finances
- – loss of income/increase in outgoings
- – increase in responsibilities
➤ Personal well being
- – health difficulties
- – emotional difficulties
➤ Development opportunities
- – for personal growth/development
➤ Physical environment
- – space, noise, light, temperature, smell, air quality, cleanliness, infestation

Key Stressor Characteristics

The impact of a stressor does not just reside in the event or the situation itself. There are other important, more qualitative aspects that are influential. Stressors pose particular difficulties for individuals when they are

➤ Felt to be out of the person's control
➤ New, not experienced before
➤ Chronic, long term
➤ Large in number
➤ Requiring rapid action

In particular the more stressors that occur together the harder the job of coping becomes. This is why work related stressors cannot be separated from stressors that arise within one's personal life—the effects are cumulative. Problems at home affect work, problems at work affect home.

When stressors impact upon an individual to create the negative mismatch referred to earlier then coping systems are set in motion.

Coping Responses

Coping is an automatic response involving four systems:

➤ Cognitive (thoughts)
➤ Emotional (feelings)
➤ Physiological (body)
➤ Behavioural (actions)

Each system affects every other system.

Cognitive

The mismatch between a perceived and a desired state generates a range of thinking processes (not necessarily or even often conscious). These include

➤ Problem solving—to find practicable ways of reducing the mismatch
➤ Reappraisal—to reduce the mismatch by
  – altering the perception of the present state (it's not as bad as I thought)
  – altering the expectation of the desired state (it didn't need to be perfect anyway)
  less helpfully, to increase the mismatch by
  – amplifying the required end state (I'll never manage that)
  – downgrading the present situation (I know nothing about handling this)

Such thinking processes will clearly affect, and be affected by, the emotions that the individual experiences.

Emotional

The negative mismatch will heighten the emotional experiences of the individual. The exact emotion will depend upon complex interactions between the nature of the problem, the prior state of the individual and the interpretations that the person makes about the situation. Experiences will include

➤ Tension
➤ Anger
➤ Fear
➤ Excitement
➤ Anxiety

Physiological

Coping responses will be represented by increases in the activity of the sympathetic nervous system. This system controls important physiological processes such as

➤ Blood pressure
➤ Heart rate
➤ Breathing
➤ Perspiration
➤ Muscle tension
➤ Gastric activity

It is an emergency system geared to enhancing short term performance by

➤ Increasing
  – blood pressure and heart rate
  – breathing rate
  – perspiration (heat loss)
  – muscle tension

➤ decreasing digestive activity

Whilst helpful in the short term, extended activation of this system can cause discomfort, distress and overt health difficulties (see below).

Behavioural

The behavioural responses to a stressful situation represent the outcome of the interchange between basic and ancient response systems (fight–flight–freeze) and later, more differentiated systems based upon learning and problem solving (stick with it—work it out).

Whilst the coping system will mean activation at all these levels the actual effectiveness of coping depends upon the resources that the individual actually has available at the time.

Coping Resources

Resources are those factors that can influence the functioning of the four coping systems. They can be divided into

Personal Resources

Resources possessed by the individual herself, including

➤ Cognitive resources
  - problem solving ability
  - flexibility
  - tolerance of ambiguity
  - self esteem
  - belief in control over events
  - religious beliefs
➤ Emotional resources
  - sense of well being
  - level of optimism
➤ Physical resources
  - general health
  - fitness
  - functioning of the immune system
  - predisposition to specific disease processes
➤ Behavioural resources
  - task specific skills
  - general social and communication skills
  - emotional management skills
➤ Financial resources—because these enable the individual to access both personal and external resources that she does not currently possess

External Resources

These are factors outside the individual which can be helpful in coping successfully with stressors. In particular other people are a key resource. Other people can provide

> Emotional support
> Problem solving support
> Task specific skills
> Practical assistance

Key sources of such support are

> At work
    – colleagues
    – supervisors
    – managers
> At home
    – partner(s)
    – friends
    – parents
    – other family members
    – neighbours
    – spiritual advisers

The Outcomes of the Coping Process

The aim of coping is to achieve a result in one or more of three areas (depending upon the nature of the situation)

> A change in the actual situation so that there is no longer a mismatch
> A change in perception of the situation so that there is no longer a mismatch
> Emotional adaptation so that the mismatch is no longer felt as disturbing (particularly important for events/situations that cannot be changed)

The coping process can result in either a positive experience (eustress) or a negative experience (distress).

Eustress

When the coping process leads to the reduction or elimination of a stressor or adaptation to it then the individual may

> Feel more skilled
> Experience a sense of personal satisfaction
> Grow in confidence and self esteem
> Be motivated to take on new/challenging tasks
> Experience a generally enhanced sense of well being

This book has been very much about how to ensure that this happens in the workplace.

Distress

Negative experiences may occur when

➤ The coping process has not succeeded in the ways outlined above
➤ The coping strategies have had to be sustained over a long period of time, even if some success has been achieved (exhaustion)
➤ The coping strategies have required action very difficult for the individual (for example, disciplinary action, making people redundant, excluding a service user)
➤ The coping strategies themselves create harm and additional stressors in the longer term (for example, high levels of alcohol consumption to relieve negative feelings, taking negative feelings out on partners or friends)

These negative experiences may be expressed in a number of ways, depending upon the individual. Distress may be evident in one or more of the four coping systems outlined earlier

➤ Cognitive
   – loss of self confidence
   – loss of self esteem
   – increased perceptions of threat (easily provoked)
   – decreased concentration span
   – forgetfulness
➤ Emotional
   – increased anxiety, tension, irritability, hopelessness
   – decreased happiness, humour, pleasure experienced
➤ Physical
   – frequent/chronic physiological signs (heart racing, sweating, muscle tension)
   – decreased immunity/poor general health
   – activation of specific physical vulnerabilities (both minor problems such as cold sores and major problems such as heart disease, cancer)
   – tiredness
   – changes in appetite (increase/decrease)
➤ Behavioural
   – increases in arguments, accidents, drug usage
   – decreases in sex, other pleasurable activities
   – changes in food intake
   – avoidance of stress provoking situations

It needs to be emphasised that the complexities involved mean that all human beings will experience distress in their lives. Distress can be minimised but it cannot be eliminated altogether. Experiencing distress is not a sign of weakness.

As can be seen from the above, the outcome of coping can generate circles of two kinds.

The virtuous circle. Successful coping creates effects that make coping with new stressors more likely to be successful. It gives the individual greater resources. A positive spiral is created.

The vicious circle. Negative outcomes create effects that reduce the likelihood of successful coping with new stressors. In addition the negative outcomes themselves may increase the number of stressors present (for example, by generating health or interpersonal difficulties). Under these conditions individuals, groups and services can be rapidly overwhelmed.

Locating this within a workplace setting suggests the need for management action at three levels—action to

➤   Promote eustress and generate virtuous circles (which is what the bulk of this book is about)
➤   Prevent distress
➤   Manage distress to prevent the development of vicious circles

IDENTIFYING DISTRESS AT WORK

At the Individual Level

The general indicators of distress have been outlined above. They will be revealed at work in a number of ways. In general

> there will be a gradual change in the behaviour of the individual

In particular the person affected will show gradual increases in one or more of the following behaviours:

➤   Taking sick leave or being absent
➤   Arriving late
➤   Forgetfulness
➤   Having accidents
➤   Making mistakes
➤   Getting into conflicts/arguments
➤   Misunderstanding things
➤   Complaining of tiredness
➤   Not making decisions
➤   Not following through on agreed action plans

This means that both the quantity and the quality of the individual's work declines as does her expressed satisfaction.

Burn Out

Closely linked to distress is the concept of burn out. This has been seen as a difficulty specific to those who engage long term in work to help others who are themselves disturbed, damaged or distressed. It has been described variously as

➢ Exhaustion from excessive demands on energy, strength or resources; or from overcommitment
➢ Withdrawal from work in response to excessive stress or dissatisfaction
➢ Progressive loss of idealism, energy and purpose
➢ Emotional exhaustion involving the development of negative self concept, negative job attitudes and loss of concern and feelings for clients

Burn out is expressed

➢ Physically
  – feelings of exhaustion and fatigue
  – lingering colds and bronchial complaints
  – headaches
  – gastrointestinal disturbances
  – sleeplessness
  – shortness of breath
  – skin complaints
  – general aches and pains
➢ Psychologically
  – touchiness and irritability
  – tearfulness
  – anger easily provoked
  – marked sadness
  – unwarranted suspiciousness
  – avoidance of commitments to caring
  – lethargy

As with any kind of distress at work burn out reflects the nature of the work itself, the conditions in the particular workplace and whatever else is going on in the person's life.

At the Group Level

If an individual is distressed this will affect that person's own work and their relationships with others at work—clients, staff, managers. Where a group or whole staff team are in distress then the sort of vicious circle described above may start to operate.

➢ The overall quality of service declines
➢ Splits, conflicts and inconsistencies increase
➢ Service users become increasingly anxious and unhappy
➢ The behaviour of service users becomes more difficult
➢ The job of the care staff now becomes more difficult

Stressors are increasing at a time when coping resources are decreasing. This kind of spiral can bring a service to crisis point in a relatively short space of time (although the build up may well have been over an extended period).

CONCLUSIONS

Care work has great potential for virtuous circles. It carries high risk for vicious circles. This book is mainly about creating the conditions in which staff function well. However, alertness is required to the risks and signs of distress and burn out so that management action can be taken to

➤ Prevent unnecessary stressors in the workplace (the job is challenging enough in itself)
➤ Equip staff with effective coping skills
➤ Identify early signs of distress and resolve the situation before it escalates
➤ Set up support systems for those who become distressed to the point that there are effects upon the quality of their work and the quality of their lives in general

The substance of this management action is the focus of the next chapter.

SUMMARY

1. STRESS IS THE EXPERIENCE OF A MISMATCH BETWEEN HOW A SITUATION IS PERCEIVED TO BE AND HOW A PERSON FEELS THE SITUATION OUGHT TO BE. THE MISMATCH IS IN A NEGATIVE DIRECTION.

2. THE EVENTS WHICH CAUSE A MISMATCH ARE CALLED STRESSORS AND EACH INDIVIDUAL HAS A NUMBER OF PERSONAL AND EXTERNAL RESOURCES WHICH CAN BE CALLED UPON TO DEAL WITH THESE STRESSORS.

3. WHEN SUFFICIENT RESOURCES EXIST TO DEAL EFFECTIVELY WITH STRESSORS THEN THE EFFECTS UPON THE INDIVIDUAL CAN BE VERY POSITIVE, WITH AN INCREASE IN CONFIDENCE, WELL BEING AND MOTIVATION ('EUSTRESS').

4. WHEN INSUFFICIENT RESOURCES EXIST, WHEN A STRESSOR GOES ON FOR TOO LONG, WHEN IT IS TOO DIFFICULT/ IMPOSSIBLE TO RESOLVE, WHEN TOO MANY STRESSORS OCCUR AT ONCE THEN THE INDIVIDUAL WILL BE OVERWHELMED AND EXPERIENCE DISTRESS. DISTRESS IS SHOWN BY SIGNS AT THE PHYSICAL, MENTAL, EMOTIONAL AND BEHAVIOURAL LEVELS. INDIVIDUALS HAVE DIFFERENT WAYS OF EXPRESSING DISTRESS.

5. THE TASK OF CARING FOR OTHERS IS RECOGNISED TO BE HIGH IN STRESSORS. CARERS ARE AT HIGH RISK FOR EXPERIENCING DISTRESS AND A PARTICULAR SYNDROME—BURN OUT—HAS BEEN DESCRIBED AND CONSIDERED COMMON IN CARE WORK.

6. DISTRESS AT BOTH THE INDIVIDUAL AND STAFF GROUP LEVEL CAN SET OFF VICIOUS CIRCLES WHICH CAN BRING STAFF MEMBERS AND SERVICES AS A WHOLE TO CRISIS POINT.

7. MANAGERS NEED TO TAKE ACTIVE STEPS TO PREVENT, IDEN-
TIFY AND RESOLVE DISTRESS AT WORK IF SERVICE QUALITY IS
TO BE SUSTAINED.

Manager's toolkit	
Tools	Applications
Knowledge about stress	Design interventions to prevent and manage stress Identify signs of distress
Observation	Identify signs of distress

CHAPTER 16   Managing stress at work

AIMS OF THE CHAPTER

1. TO CONSIDER HOW DISTRESS AT WORK CAN BE PREVENTED BY IDENTIFYING, MANAGING OR ELIMINATING STRESSORS.

2. TO CONSIDER THE SKILLS AND SUPPORTS WHICH ARE NEEDED BY CAREGIVERS IF THEY ARE TO DEAL EFFECTIVELY WITH THE STRESSORS THAT THEY ENCOUNTER.

3. TO CONSIDER THE SUPPORTS WHICH CAN BE SET UP IN THE WORKPLACE TO HELP THOSE CAREGIVERS WHO EXPERIENCE SIGNIFICANT DISTRESS.

INTRODUCTION

A comprehensive approach to stress and distress at work is underpinned by the following principles:

1. Team and individual functioning are interdependent.
2. If individuals are functioning well, physically and psychologically, then the team and, ultimately, the organisation for which they work is likely to
   - work effectively
   - deliver a quality service
   And (conversely . . .)
3. Managers have a responsibility for the functioning of individual staff members and thereby the working team.
4. By taking steps to promote the physical and psychological well being of each individual within the organisation managers enhance the quality of the work produced by the individual and by the working team.
5. Individual, team and organisational distress are not inevitable.
6. Despite the high level of stressors present within care work a great deal can be done to reduce the negative impact of these upon individuals and thereby the team and the organisation as a whole.
7. Individuals, teams and organisations cope and react in varied ways to stress. Levels of stress found acceptable vary across
   - individuals
   - teams
   - organisations
   Coping strategies will vary likewise as will the resources available and the history of

coping. Distress too will show itself in different ways. An understanding of these differences will be vital to the identification of difficulties.

8. Individuals and teams develop and change. Both the stressors at work and the resources available vary over time. Attention to workplace stress is an ongoing process not something that is dealt with once and for all.

The effective management of stress within the workplace requires a comprehensive approach, with activity at three levels.

LEVEL 1: THE PREVENTION OF AVOIDABLE STRESS

Work at this level is directed at controlling the number and intensity of stressors. The aim is to create the optimum degree of stress so that the staff feel

challenged

but

not overwhelmed

As already mentioned the bulk of this book is about maximising such positive functioning in the workplace. This section of the chapter will refer to many topics covered elsewhere in the book. Unless there is anything new to add, readers will be referred to the relevant chapters.

Stressors can arise from a number of sources:

The Work Itself

Knowing What is Expected

Uncertainty—not being clear about what tasks one is expected to do—can be a major stressor. Clear job descriptions and performance objectives (see Chapter 5) contribute to positive motivation. The lack of them will create demotivation and stress as individuals struggle with

➤ Not knowing what is expected
➤ Having no yardstick against which to evaluate performance

The Volume of Work

The ideal is to ensure that staff are busy but not overloaded. Whilst workload cannot always be controlled by management action (as with emergencies, staff shortages) Chapter 10 covers a number of ways in which steps can be taken to

➤ Set priorities
➤ Manage time

This will be a recurring activity as resources may vary over time—it is important to keep the balance so that the amount and complexity of the work asked of staff is realistic in terms of the resources available. This of course generates a whole other sphere of activity for the readers of this book—extracting from senior management additional resources to match the goals being set for a service.

The Complexity of Work

Work needs to be challenging but not overwhelming. Training (see Chapter 9) has a key role in ensuring that staff have the knowledge and skills to actually do the job that is being asked of them.

Role Factors

Uncertainty

In any service there are different types of job that need doing. Stress can arise when

> a staff member is not clear about the type of job that she is supposed to do

She may be quite capable of each job individually but remains uncertain as to which of the many jobs available is truly hers to do.

Example

A deputy team leader in a residential home finds that she is expected by colleagues to take a full and active part in the direct care of service users. Her manager, however, expects her to spend more time in the office sorting out the paperwork and dealing with administrative matters. This leads to hassle from the manager when she spends a lot of time with service users, hassle from the staff when she spends time in the office.

Conflict

In the above example the resolution is to sort out the balance in jobs and time allocation. Sometimes, however, role difficulties present more as direct conflicts than uncertainty.

Example

A manager finds that she is placed in the role of counsellor by staff, who come to her with their personal difficulties and rely on her confidentiality. However, she also has to ensure that staff performance does not fall below acceptable standards. If it does she will need to take corrective or disciplinary action . . . with the very people whom she counsels about personal difficulties that she knows have an influence upon their functioning at work.

Another kind of conflict situation arises where job requirements conflict with personal beliefs.

Example

An individual believes that those who are the victims of violence are entitled to retribution. Working in a service where users sometimes act in dangerous ways towards others, he finds that not only must he take no steps towards retribution but that he is also expected to counsel those who behave in such ways.

Dealing with Role Difficulties

There are a number of management interventions that can help avoid or resolve role difficulties:

➤ Establishing clear, realistic job descriptions
➤ Supervision
➤ Training

There are also some specific role clarification exercises (see Tables 16.1 and 16.2).

Dealing with role issues is therefore another important contributor to managing stressors and preventing distress.

Control Factors

In so far as staff feel unable to control or to influence events that happen at work, they experience

➤ At best—demotivation
➤ At worst—distress

Whilst there will be many factors over which staff can exert little influence it is vital to identify those areas over which control is possible . . . and to delegate that control to staff. This issue is discussed more fully in Chapter 4.

The Physical Environment

Stressors arise from the physical environment, to affect staff and service users.

Noise

Excessive noise can affect hearing. It will certainly interfere with verbal communication. Certain types of noise will be in and of themselves unpleasant, sometimes to the point of physical pain.

Table 16.1 Exercise: clarifying the 'carer' role

This is carried out with a staff group and takes about one hour

Step 1: Warm up
        Staff discuss the job of 'carer'—the things that are:
        easy
        hard
        unexpected

Step 2: Identifying the roles in being a 'carer'
        The group brainstorm the roles they fulfil in the course of their work—roles such as:
        teacher
        friend
        advocate
        coach
        minder
        helper

Step 3: Role examination
        Each individual identifies the roles that she finds easy and those that she finds difficult.
        The group discusses the reasons for finding particular roles easy or hard

Step 4: Identifying core difficulties
        The group discusses whether they find any two roles particularly difficult to switch in
        and out of, and the reasons underlying such difficulty

Step 5: Resolving core difficulties
        Where specific roles have been identified as difficult or role pairs as difficult to fulfil at
        the same time (for example, teacher and friend), the group seeks a resolution. This may
        mean:
        discarding certain roles
        altering their definition
        assigning priorities more clearly

Step 6: Overview of session
        The complexities and conflicts in the carer role are summarised. The solutions arrived at
        are identified and spelled out in terms of their practical implications

Examples

A day facility for people with learning diffi-culties was set up in an old hall which had a very high ceiling. The many windows had no curtains. The floor was covered in linoleum. Chairs and tables had metal legs which scraped on the floor as they were moved. The table tops were metal and resounded whenever a hard object was placed upon them. Voices were distorted and magnified so that it was sometimes difficult to hear what was being said by someone only a few feet away. Staff complained of headaches and irritability. Service users were always irri-table and levels of disruptive behaviour were high.

One of the six people living in a small com-munity home squealed in a very high pitch. Without verbal communication this individ-ual squealed to express pleasure, distress and boredom. Sometimes the sound was emitted just for the sheer joy of making it. However, one man's meat . . . the sound caused irritation and stress to anyone else who had to spend more than half an hour continually in her presence. It was always no-ticeable that the behaviour of other res-idents was much calmer when this individual was out.

Table 16.2 Exercise: clarifying role in a team context (from Dayal and Thomas, 1968)

This exercise is relevant in a team where members have differing roles.

Step 1
The person whose job role is being analysed defines (on a flip chart/whiteboard/OHP)
— the tasks/actions that make up the role
— how the role relates to other roles in the team
— how the role helps the team achieves its functions.

Step 2
The rest of the team add or remove points until the whole group, including the individual concerned, are satisfied that the role is comprehensively defined.

Step 3
The individual identifies her expectations of the other roles within the team, particularly those that are most closely linked to her being able to do the job outlined in Step 1.

Step 4
Other team members list out how they would like to see the person whose role is being analysed function.

Step 5
Both lists are discussed and modified until they are agreed upon by the whole group.

Step 6
The individual whose role is being analysed makes a written summary of the role as defined in the previous steps. This summary is presented subsequently to the team for final agreement.

This exercise can be repeated with each key role in the team

Controlling noise may be a matter of:

➣ Engineering—buffers, sound proofing etc.
➣ Behaviour change—helping an individual to reduce their noise level
➣ Practical management—minimising the exposure of individuals to irritating/unpleasant noises

Smell

Unpleasant and strong smells can be a source of irritation and constitute an additional stressor. Incontinence is an obvious example but there may be others related to external pollutants or to personal hygiene in general. Again the atmospheric interventions may be seen in terms of:

➣ Engineering—ventilation, air freshening/filtering etc.
➣ Behaviour change—improving continence, personal hygiene
➣ Practical management—minimising exposure

Space

Small settings, particularly if staffed, are often very limited in the amount of space available. It may be very hard for both users and providers to find somewhere quiet and private to go to when necessary (for example, to concentrate on an activity, to recover from upset)

This is particularly problematic if behaviour disturbances occur. In all environments there should be a place designated where

clients and staff can go to when things get too much or some peace and quiet is needed

Temperature

The ability to control the temperature in an environment so that it is not too hot and not too cold is another way of preventing unnecessary stressors. Individual tolerances and preferences vary greatly in this respect. The solutions are at two levels:

> ➤ Engineering—local control of heating and ventilation systems
> ➤ Practical management—clothing to maintain the individual at an optimal level of comfort

Personal Development Opportunities

Lack of scope for personal growth and development will be demotivating for many people. For those people to whom such development is central, lack of scope is more frustrating and comes to constitute a positive stressor. The steps to prevention in this area are covered in Chapter 6.

Organisational/Team Change

Change, like all stressors, offers the possibility of growth or distress. Lack of change is equally 'risky' from this point of view. This is a massive area on which a whole separate literature exists. However, when change is planned or under way a number of interventions will help to avoid the experience of distress.

Information

Keeping individuals and teams informed about

> ➤ What is happening
> ➤ The reasons for change
> ➤ The people likely to be affected by change
> ➤ The possible problems with the implementation of the changes
> ➤ The timetable for change

Where no new information is available this also should be conveyed (silence is often seen in these circumstances as meaning active concealment).

The information needs to be

➤ Conveyed in different formats (newsletters, briefings, question and answer sessions, videos)
➤ Repeated to make sure that it is understood, remembered, interpreted correctly

Training

If the changes mean that staff require new attitudes, knowledge and/or skills training will have a key contribution.

Encouragement

Thought will need to be given to increasing the level of encouragement offered to staff for adopting new patterns of behaviour at work (see Chapters 11, 12, 13).

Participation

The more individuals and teams can be given influence in the change process (goals, methods, timing) the greater the likelihood of ownership and the less the likelihood of distress.

Emotional Support

The need for emotional support will be higher at times of change—there will be a general need for more listening. Increasing the opportunities for staff to be heard and to express their feelings in safety will help to prevent distress. This may be effected by

➤ Increasing the frequency of supervision
➤ Increasing the frequency of group meetings
➤ Establishing a time limited support group (see below)

All these provide ways in to making change a constructive rather than a destructive process.

LEVEL 2: ENHANCING COPING MECHANISMS

Work at this level

➤ Identifies stressors
➤ Ensures that coping resources—both personal and external—are used effectively;

And . . . if possible

➤ Enhances those resources

It maximises the likelihood that staff will cope constructively with the stressors that inevitably arise in care work. Three types of management activity contribute to this process:

Training Programmes in Coping Competences

Knowledge and skill in a number of areas contribute to effective responding in the face of stressors.

General Stress Management Training

Although programmes will vary to some extent, content should enable individuals to learn to

➤ Recognise the stressors which are affecting them
➤ Understand the effects of the stressor on the four response systems—feelings, thoughts, behaviours and physiological systems
➤ Recognise the unhelpful/harmful coping strategies that they are using
➤ Identify the personal and interpersonal coping resources which are available to them
➤ Learn a variety of techniques which can be used to reduce the potentially harmful effects of stressors:
  – appropriate expression of emotion
  – appropriate use of support networks
  – reconstruction of unhelpful beliefs/interpretations of events
  – positive thinking about oneself and about the events that are going on
➤ Learn new skills which can be added to the individual's stock of personal resources for reducing the number of stressors operating in life:
  – physical relaxation skills
  – assertiveness skills
  – lifestyle management skills
➤ Use a problem solving approach to select and implement the most appropriate strategies for coping successfully with a particular stressor, based upon the analysis described above

Stress management training is about helping the individual to act effectively and to take at least some control of difficult situations by

➤ Altering that situation
➤ Construing the situation in a way that makes it easier to tolerate
➤ Expressing emotions in a constructive way

As well as this general approach to stress management, training can be directed to some of the specific skills mentioned above.

Lifestyle Management

This starts from the premise that distress is the result of

➤ The cumulative experience of stressors in work and in personal life
➤ Failing to take care of the underlying personal coping systems

Lifestyle management suggests that well being requires a balance between the time and energy spent

at work and at home

on positive activities and on problems.

It helps participants to

➤ Set goals for themselves in their personal life:
 – to prioritise these
 – to break them down into smaller achievable steps
 – to work systematically towards achieving them
➤ Schedule time for recreation and leisure
➤ Take care of their body through exercise and diet
➤ *Not* feel guilty about relaxing and doing nothing in one's own time

Assertiveness Training

Assertiveness in general is about

➤ Confronting problems at the time that they occur in order to avoid the build up of negative feelings
➤ Managing conflicts to seek a negotiated outcome

Assertiveness training in particular is about the skills involved in

➤ Dealing with confrontations
➤ Saying 'No'
➤ Handling compliments and criticisms
➤ Expressing negative and positive feelings
➤ Expressing personal opinions

It teaches participants to

➤ Examine their motives in interpersonal interactions and their beliefs about themselves and their world
➤ Consider how these beliefs and motives influence their interpersonal style
➤ Recognise the situations when assertive messages should be used
➤ Practise communicating assertively in a range of situations

Assertiveness is a key set of skills for working in team settings as these require

➤ Team effort and consistency
➤ A high level of effective communication between team members

Relaxation Training

Relaxation training focusses upon the physiological and emotional response to situations. It teaches participants to

➤ Recognise when and how their body responds with physical tension to situations
➤ Use a set of skills to control this response

There are a number of strategies for effecting a calmer state, including

➤ Progressive muscular relaxation
➤ Yoga
➤ Meditation

All of the above training inputs can be provided by

➤ External trainers/consultants
➤ The many open courses in this area, both in the professional and in the public domain

There are also many self help books, manuals, audio and video tapes available. It is hoped that the above will assist managers in

➤ Designing their own programmes
➤ Judging the quality of external training offered
➤ Advising staff seeking personal development in this area

Promoting Social Support Networks Within the Organisation

Social supports provide an important buffer against the negative effects of stress. The support of another can help an individual to

➤ Work through negative emotions
➤ See a situation from a different perspective
➤ Generate new solutions to a problem
➤ Receive encouragement to use existing coping strategies
➤ Receive practical help with specific tasks
➤ Feel valued
➤ Maintain a positive self image

Social support at work can be promoted in a number of ways:

Informal Networks

Staff may well develop their own support networks—for example, over cups of tea, lunch, a drink in the pub after work. Attention to team development (see Chapter 7) will raise the likelihood of this happening. However, relying entirely upon such a system may leave a number of staff unsupported.

➤ Some individuals may not want to burden colleagues with their own difficulties

➤ Others may fear that admitting to difficulties will make them seem weak or inadequate

Staff Meetings

Where regular staff meetings take place, time can be set aside for issues which are causing stress within a team. Such time is most likely to be well spent if the issues to be discussed are

agreed in advance of the meeting

This gives participants time to think about the issues and their contribution to the discussion. The discussion itself will require careful management so that time is not just spent 'moaning'; but that problem solving is used to

➤ Improve the situation
➤ Alter perceptions of the situation
➤ Reduce high levels of emotion

Buddy System

This is an organised but informal system of support, particularly useful for new staff. Following the appointment of a new staff member a 'buddy' is there to help the new staff member through at least the first several months of the job:

➤ To answer queries
➤ To help deal with minor problems

Contact is made before the new person starts and a meeting arranged as soon as possible after commencement. Thereafter the two meet by mutual arrangement.

In addition to these rather 'loose' approaches to the enhancement of social support mechanisms there are more formal management interventions to promote effective coping.

Formal Management Interventions

Staff Supervision

Regular supervision provides a net for the early detection of coping difficulties experienced by staff around work related issues. It provides a forum to discuss how difficulties can be

➤ Resolved (appropriate action taken)
➤ Adapted to (perceptions altered)

Good supervision will also teach staff PROBLEM ANALYSIS and PROBLEM SOLVING SKILLS which they can apply to new problems as they arise (further reducing the risk of stress). A problem solving format adapted to stress related issues is outlined in Table 16.3.

Table 16.3 A problem solving approach to dealing with stressors

1. Define precisely the nature of the stressor
2. Identify the effects of the stressor on the individual (emotions, thoughts and beliefs, behaviour, physiology)
3. Can the stressor or the distress caused by it be eliminated or reduced by thinking about the situation in a different way? How?
4. Can the stressor or the distress caused by it be eliminated or reduced by doing something positive about the situation? What?
5. Can the person do something to make himself less upset or angry about the situation? What?
6. Decide which of the above would be the most helpful and which are achievable
7. Agree a plan of action
8. Review actions taken at a later date

Staff Support Groups

Staff support groups may be made available to individual work teams or be offered across work teams, drawing members from different areas of service provision.

Staff support groups can serve a number of functions in relation to stress. They may consider

➤ Work related stressors that group members face (for example, violence at work, dealing with relatives of clients)
➤ Stressors arising outside work (for example, being a single parent)
➤ Interprofessional conflict

Staff groups give members time and space to

➤ Work through individual problems
➤ Learn from each other

Such groups must

➤ Have a clear set of aims
➤ Have a clear set of ground rules
➤ Meet regularly for an agreed time period
➤ Be led by a skilled facilitator

If use of a staff group is to be considered for a single working team then

attendance will need to be compulsory

Otherwise the group itself may split the team or feed splits already present.

Thus there are many ways in which the coping resources of staff can be maximised and distress reduced or prevented. However, situations will arise when prevention and constructive coping fail and the manager is faced with staff in distress.

LEVEL 3: MANAGING DISTRESS

Work at this level is directed at providing help for the individual or team experiencing distress, to

➤ Alleviate discomfort
➤ Restore well being and effective functioning

For the individual concerned this means medical or psychological help. For the team suffering distress this means team crisis intervention.

Managing Individual Distress

The manager's role here is to

> effect referral to appropriate medical or psychological resources

or to

> press the organisation to make provision for such contingencies

Medical or psychological help may be provided 'in house', with the doctor or psychologist/counsellor/therapist employed by the organisation. Staff may

➤ Refer themselves directly
➤ Be referred by the manager when problems are identified and criteria for negative impact on work performance are met (for example, alcohol difficulties which lead to frequent absences from work or which impair on the job work functioning)

An explicit policy on confidentiality is essential.

Alternatively provision for medical or psychological care can be made with independent providers. Staff are given information about the service and how to access it (access has to be direct). Such 'off line/off site' services are sometimes preferred because in addition to the general issue of confidentiality individuals have the extra security of knowing that no-one else need be aware that they are receiving professional help.

Such services are time limited and crisis oriented. Where individuals require more extensive help with problems then referral is made to mainstream health provision.

A programme of medical or psychological assistance to individuals within an organisation is more likely to be used effectively if

➤ There is a clear set of policies and procedures outlining the purpose of the service
➤ Supervisors/managers are trained in problem identification
➤ There is a programme of education for employees and promotion of the service within the organisation
➤ There is an explicit policy of confidentiality

Managing a Team's Distress

Where a team is clearly in distress then the intervention of an independent consultant skilled in group work may be helpful. This will supplement the support services to individual team members outlined above. The consultant works with the team and with individual team members to help them to identify and to resolve their own problems by

➤ Making them aware of the processes at work and their effects
➤ Making them aware of the mechanisms which can be used to effect change
➤ Facilitating the change process itself

CONCLUSIONS

Stress within the workplace cannot be avoided. Indeed a certain level of stress is helpful in challenging and motivating staff. However, some stress is unnecessary—the job itself is difficult enough without added burdens. Too much stress is potentially harmful to

➤ The individuals affected
➤ The working team
➤ The organisation as a whole

And thereby to

➤ The users of the service

Active management is therefore necessary to

➤ Prevent unnecessary stress
➤ Enhance coping with inevitable stress
➤ Relieve acute distress

SUMMARY

1. INDIVIDUAL, TEAM AND ORGANISATIONAL HEALTH ARE INTERDEPENDENT.

2. REDUCING THE PROBABILITY OF NEGATIVE IMPACTS OF STRESS REQUIRES THE ELIMINATION OF UNNECESSARY STRESSORS.

3. INDIVIDUAL COPING CAN BE ENHANCED BY TRAINING IN STRESS MANAGEMENT AND RELATED SKILLS.

4. INDIVIDUAL AND TEAM COPING CAN BE ENHANCED BY THE DEVELOPMENT AND MAINTENANCE OF SOCIAL SUPPORT NETWORKS WITHIN THE WORKPLACE.

5. MANAGERS NEED TO BE ALERT TO EARLY SIGNS OF DISTRESS AND TO ACTIVELY SEEK TO ALLEVIATE THIS BY JOINT PROBLEM

SOLVING BASED UPON A SHARED UNDERSTANDING OF THE
PROCESS OF STRESS AND COPING. SUPERVISION AND STAFF
SUPPORT GROUPS ARE MECHANISMS FOR EFFECTING THIS.

6. THERE WILL BE A NEED FOR CRISIS INTERVENTION SERVICES
   TO SUPPORT INDIVIDUALS AND TEAMS IN ACUTE DISTRESS.
   THIS WILL INVOLVE MEDICAL AND/OR PSYCHOLOGICAL HELP.

Manager's toolkit	
Tools	Applications
Role analysis/writing job descriptions	Set clear expectations for staff
Prioritising	Set realistic goals for staff
Time management	Set realistic goals for staff
Identifying training needs	Equip staff with job competence. Equip staff with stress management competence
Supervision	Set clear expectations for staff. Detect signs of distress. Help problem solving around stress related issues
Problem solving	Improve individual/team coping with stress related issues. Identify and resolve environmental contributions to stress
Observation	Identify environmental contributions to stress. Identify signs of distress in staff
Communicating information	Reduce impact of organisational change
Giving encouragement/positive feedback	Reduce impact of organisational change
Delegation/increase participation	Reduce impact of organisational change
Listening/offer support	Reduce impact of organisational change
Managing meetings	Enable staff to discuss and problem solve stress related issues
Team building	Promote informal social support networks
Setting briefs/contracting	Manage use of external trainers/consultants
Referring on	Get effective professional help to staff in distress

SECTION V   **Final Thoughts**

CHAPTER 17   **What about me?**

AIMS OF THE CHAPTER

1. To reinforce the relevance of the book to a manager's own satisfaction and performance.

2. To identify ways in which a manager can act to develop conditions which maximise her own satisfaction and performance.

INTRODUCTION

Those in middle management positions, the intended readership of this book, can be amongst the most stressed group of employees within an organisation. They often

➤ Work in relative isolation
➤ Have to deal with pressures coming up from staff
➤ Have to deal with pressures coming down from senior management

The demands from both levels can be high and conflicting.

In terms of service quality the success of the middle management process is critical. Thus care over the functioning of middle managers should be a major consideration in services for those with long term disabilities. Yet, in our experience, this is all too rarely the case. Middle managers often experience

      high levels of stress

and

      low levels of support

with results damaging to

      themselves
      their staff
      the service users

The principles and practices outlined in this book are 'universals'. That is, they reflect what is known about the factors that influence human behaviour . . . in general. Whilst the book focusses upon their application to the behaviour of care staff, the principles and practices are equally applicable to the functioning of managers in such services.

However, given the shortcomings in many service situations, the present chapter looks at what managers can do to develop working conditions that will maximise their own functioning

IDENTIFYING PERSONAL NEEDS

The first step is to pinpoint the factors conducive to good functioning that are most lacking in the manager's current work situation. The checklist in Appendix 1 can be used for this purpose, completed in terms of the conditions that apply to the manager herself.

This will provide an overview of the current situation from a motivation/performance perspective. From it can be extracted a list of

what is not available from whom

Ordering this in terms of personal priorities gives an

agenda for action

IDENTIFYING BLOCKS

The present situation in which a manager finds himself will not have arisen by chance. It is therefore important to identify factors that

➤ Contribute to the status quo
➤ Block important developments

These factors may lie within

➤ The individual manager
➤ The employing organisation
➤ The broader social/political system

Given the nature of this book, only the first two areas will be considered.

Personal Blocks

There are a number of blocks that may lie within the individual that may contribute to a perpetuation of the status quo, unsatisfactory though it may seem. For example, seeking a change in the present situation may be blocked by

➤ Anxiety, about asserting oneself in general
➤ A wish to please and be liked at all costs which means avoiding causing upset to others at all costs
➤ A wish to be seen as perfect and in control which makes it hard to discuss things that are not satisfactory

A highly stressed situation at work may be maintained because it is a means of

➤ Getting excitement

➤ Maintaining a role of being the hero underdog taking on all the world's problems
➤ Maintaining a victim role, that safe situation where one has no influence over all the things that are wrong, they are all the fault of someone else over whom one has no control
➤ Remaining all absorbed with work, which avoids facing problems in other areas of life

The reader will need to look long and hard at himself to see if any of these (or other personal) factors apply. If they do then they will need to be addressed in their own right if change is to occur. The detailed methods for changing these personal blocks are beyond the scope of this book, although some will have been alluded to in Section IV.

Environmental Blocks

Important sources of motivation and performance support may be lacking because the organisation as a whole has not formulated policies and working procedures in relevant areas.

> there may be no organisational approach to mission statements, supervision and appraisal systems, performance related pay and conditions

Another block may be actual lack of resources.

> there may be very limited budgetary allocation for training or environmental upgrading

These are two common blocks. They may be difficult to remove and the choice for the manager is

➤ Try to change organisational policies and budgetary allocations as a whole
➤ Try to effect some immediate change to improve personal circumstances (set up a personal supervision system with the immediate line manager, squeeze an individual sum of money to support a personal training input)

Given the immediacy of the needs the latter might be preferable. However, in the long run any such individual arrangement will be fragile unless more general changes are effected. So at some point the broader issues will need to be addressed . . . but perhaps not first off.

INTERVENTIONS FOR CHANGE

There are a number of avenues that can be explored in order to effect change in the conditions at work. The exact route to be followed will be determined by

➤ The change required
➤ Individual preferences
➤ Past experience of trying to effect change

Assert for Change in . . . (Senior) Manager Behaviour

Change may be effected by assertive communication upwards to senior management

indicating what is wanted . . . and why

This would be the most effective route for a large number of changes. Senior management should be the source of

➤ Goal setting
➤ Feedback
➤ Supervision and support
➤ Appraisal
➤ Clarification of service purpose
➤ Involvement in decision making

This book is about the conditions that management can create in order to influence satisfaction and performance . . . it is irrelevant whether the consumer of the management process is a direct caregiver or the leader of a staff group.

Effect Change in . . . Staff Behaviour

Staff may be particularly helpful in providing feedback on manager behaviour. This may occur spontaneously (not unfailingly constructive); or it may be necessary to develop structures to facilitate the process.

Rating forms could be developed for items such as supervision sessions or meetings so that the manager gets feedback on areas that reflect her performance.

Staff could be asked to record the number of times that they receive positive and critical feedback.

Service review activities could involve evaluation of the management process that staff receive.

In these ways staff can provide valuable feedback on manager behaviour that will influence motivation and performance.

Self Help . . . Develop a Network

In many areas of life people access support by joining together with others who are in a similar position or who share similar interests. First line managers are often

➤ Socially isolated from others working in similar positions
➤ Caught between the pressures from staff and from senior management

Setting up a group for local managers working in the same or similar organisations may serve as an important source of support. In particular it may help with

➤ Emotional support for stress related difficulties
➤ Practical problem solving in relation to service issues
➤ The development of relevant training

Self Help . . . Self Management

There is much that individuals can do to influence for themselves their own motivation and behaviour. This is true in all areas of life and can be readily applied to manager functioning. Examples include:

➤ Setting and monitoring realistic goals for oneself
➤ Giving oneself feedback including setting up 'contracts' with oneself that makes a specific reward dependent upon the achievement of specific goals
➤ Writing prioritised 'to-do' lists
➤ Identifying positive aspects of oneself and the working situation

These are all viable ways of influencing one's own motivation and behaviour.

Chapter 16 indicated a range of personal competences that are useful in buffering against distress and demotivation. These competences can be accessed via self help manuals or open courses.

These are all examples of self management towards optimising one's own motivation and behaviour.

CONCLUSIONS

This chapter is not intended as a comprehensive overview of manager motivation and performance. Rather it seeks to stress the point that the motivation and performance of managers is influenced by exactly the same variables that influence staff motivation and performance. If the best is wanted from its managers an organisation must create the conditions that enable them to give of their best.

In practice many organisations fail in this respect. Thus the chapter has sought also to indicate practical ways in which managers might act to create conditions that enable them to function well. The methods described are not mutually exclusive and the combination chosen will reflect the individual conditions that a manager finds herself in. There are probably other approaches that the individual reader will think of. The key point is that it will be hard for managers to take care of their staff if they themselves are not taken care of.

SUMMARY

1. THE EFFECTIVE FUNCTIONING OF MIDDLE MANAGERS IS AN IMPORTANT DETERMINANT OF SERVICE QUALITY.

2. THE PRINCIPLES AND PRACTICES DESCRIBED IN THIS BOOK ARE AS RELEVANT TO THE FUNCTIONING OF MANAGERS AS THEY ARE TO THE FUNCTIONING OF STAFF.

3. THE QUALITY OF MANAGER MANAGEMENT IS OFTEN POOR IN HUMAN SERVICES.

4. THE INDIVIDUAL MANAGER WHO WISHES TO CHANGE THE CONDITIONS WHICH INFLUENCE HER OWN SATISFACTION AND PERFORMANCE NEEDS FIRST TO IDENTIFY PRIORITY AREAS FOR ACTION.

5. BLOCKS TO CHANGE WITHIN ONESELF AND/OR THE WORKING ENVIRONMENT SHOULD BE ADDRESSED.

6. CHANGE CAN BE EFFECTED BY ASSERTIVE COMMUNICATION TO SENIOR MANAGEMENT.

7. STAFF CAN BE A VALUABLE SOURCE OF FEEDBACK BUT THIS WILL NEED STRUCTURING IF MAXIMUM BENEFIT IS TO BE GAINED.

8. GENERAL SUPPORT, PROBLEM SOLVING AND TRAINING MAY BE IMPROVED BY NETWORKING WITH FELLOW MANAGERS.

9. THERE ARE SELF MANAGEMENT TACTICS WHICH WILL CONTRIBUTE TO SATISFACTION AND PERFORMANCE—GOAL SETTING, SELF FEEDBACK, TIME MANAGEMENT, POSITIVE THINKING, STRESS MANAGEMENT.

Manager's toolkit	
Tools	Applications
Problem solving	Identify blocks to change, set up manager network, develop stress buffering lifestyles
Assertiveness	Effect change in the behaviour of senior management and staff
Design rating scales/questionnaires	Elicit constructive feedback from staff
Goal setting	Improve own performance
Feedback	Improve own performance/satisfaction
Time management	Improve own performance/satisfaction
Stress management	Improve personal well being

CONCLUDING REMARKS

IS THAT ALL THERE IS TO IT?

This book has had a limited focus:

➤ It is about care services as they are currently constituted in the society in which the authors live
➤ It is by psychologists and about psychological approaches to the management process
➤ It has tried to describe practical approaches to everyday problems

It has not sought

➤ To address the deeper issues that arise in caring for damaged people in a society that devalues the imperfect
➤ To give a comprehensive overview of all psychological theories that have been applied to the workplace
➤ To be a comprehensive guide to management (in particular the whole area of financial/material resource management has been excluded)

It has been driven by the authors' own experiences and beliefs . . . in particular that

➤ There are many examples in care services of people doing the best they can with the resources that they have
➤ There are many examples in care services of people not doing the best they can with the resources that they have
➤ The gap between the first two points can be bridged very often by the relatively straightforward interventions that this book has tried to itemise

We believe very firmly that people with long term disabilities can be offered services that are and remain of high quality . . . and that they should have every reason to expect such services.

WHERE TO START

With the above in mind the question then arises about where to start with the improvement process. The first step is to analyse the present state of the service that you are managing from the perspective on which this book has concentrated. The checklist in Appendix 1 can help with this.

The assessment should be summarised in terms of

➤ The changes that appear most urgently needed

➤   The changes that would have the greatest overall impact
➤   The changes that you feel most able to effect
➤   The changes that you feel most comfortable with effecting

The decision on where to start is then a judgement call. Our own preferences are to make change slowly and to start with the changes that you feel most able to effect and comfortable about. These would constitute the short term goals. However, if left at that it may mean that important but difficult and uncomfortable changes are avoided. Thus it is vital that these changes are targeted for action and entered into a timetable for change— the goal is identified and a date attached! This keeps them in view and gives time for preparation that might make the changes easier and more comfortable to implement.

Good luck . . . and if in doubt look to the stars

APPENDIX 1 Checklist for analysing personal performance as a STAR manager

THE STAR MANAGER

This rating scale will help you to appraise yourself and your service in relation to those management activities which contribute to the positive performance and morale of staff. It is a job aid rather than a validated measurement device. No one individual and no service could be expected to function excellently in all areas. Likewise areas of need highlighted should not be seen as faults but as spurs to improvement; and of course whether such improvement occurs is not just the responsibility of the individual manager.

Performance is rated on a four point scale.

1. *Not at all.* The area in question is not addressed in any way.
2. *Could do better.* The area in question is addressed but improvements could be made. To rate at this level you must know what specifically could be done to improve matters.
3. *Good enough.* You do this as well as any other ordinary person/service. You may think that things could be better but you cannot identify specifically how such improvements could be made.
4. *Excellent.* This is a real area of strength for you/your service.

Rate each statement by circling the number that best describes the current situation. At the end of the form identify specific areas of strength and need. Then outline specific targets for improvement and how such improvement might be brought about.

1. I know what motivates my staff	1	2	3	4
2. Our service has a clear sense and statement of purpose (mission)	1	2	3	4
3. Staff know and understand the service mission	1	2	3	4
4. The mission statement is referred to in the course of decision making	1	2	3	4
5. I meet regularly with my staff	1	2	3	4
6. Staff participate in making the decisions about the work that they do	1	2	3	4
7. I and my staff engage in joint problem solving	1	2	3	4
8. In our work we look at strengths and successes as well as needs and difficulties	1	2	3	4

9. I and my staff talk about things that are going well	1	2	3	4
10. I challenge staff who make unhelpful attributions	1	2	3	4
11. My staff have clear goals in their work	1	2	3	4
12. My staff have realistic goals	1	2	3	4
13. We review goals that are set	1	2	3	4
14. We have an individual planning system for service users	1	2	3	4
15. We have an individual planning system for staff	1	2	3	4
16. My staff have clear, realistic job descriptions	1	2	3	4
17. I have contact with my staff during the course of their everyday work	1	2	3	4
18. I show staff ways of working with clients and ways of problem solving	1	2	3	4
19. I give staff feedback on how they carry out work tasks	1	2	3	4
20. Staff are given projects to work on	1	2	3	4
21. Staff have access to information on new developments in the field	1	2	3	4
22. Staff have access to training	1	2	3	4
23. We have an appraisal system for staff	1	2	3	4
24. We have a supervision system for staff	1	2	3	4
25. We have a training policy	1	2	3	4
26. I know what are my staff's training needs	1	2	3	4
27. I ensure that staff receive training in line with their needs	1	2	3	4
28. We have a stated philosophy that emphasises teamwork	1	2	3	4
29. We have agreed ground rules about behaviour at work	1	2	3	4
30. As a staff group we communicate openly and honestly	1	2	3	4
31. We engage in specific activities to strengthen team functioning	1	2	3	4
32. We review how we work together as a team	1	2	3	4
33. We take active steps to manage conflicts between ourselves	1	2	3	4
34. I monitor the language used to talk about service users	1	2	3	4
35. We look at strengths before needs	1	2	3	4
36. We use objective information systems to support decision making	1	2	3	4
37. I take conscious steps to fire up the positive motivation of my staff	1	2	3	4
38. Staff have access to effective training	1	2	3	4
39. Staff acquire the knowledge, skills and values that they need to do their job well	1	2	3	4
40. We make use of open learning approaches to training	1	2	3	4
41. Tasks/goals are prioritised	1	2	3	4

42. I manage actively time allocation to tasks	1	2	3	4
43. Tasks are allocated to specific people	1	2	3	4
44. There are salient cues to remind staff about day to day work	1	2	3	4
45. Work is timetabled	1	2	3	4
46. There are written programme plans	1	2	3	4
47. We monitor and review time allocation	1	2	3	4
48. We have attainable performance standards	1	2	3	4
49. Staff receive structured, objective feedback about their work efforts	1	2	3	4
50. Staff have visual feedback (e.g. graphs) on their work	1	2	3	4
51. I myself give staff structured, objective feedback about their work efforts	1	2	3	4
52. I praise/thank my staff for their work	1	2	3	4
53. I sometimes give positive feedback when I notice staff acting appropriately	1	2	3	4
54. We practise giving and receiving social reinforcement	1	2	3	4
55. We have means of publicly recognising good performance	1	2	3	4
56. I give clear feedback to my staff when they have acted in unacceptable/unskilled ways	1	2	3	4
57. My staff gain material benefits from functioning well	1	2	3	4
58. I monitor staff for signs of distress	1	2	3	4
59. I ensure that staff do not experience role uncertainty or role conflict	1	2	3	4
60. I ensure that the physical environment at work is not a source of discomfort	1	2	3	4
61. I take active steps to minimise the negative effects of change	1	2	3	4
62. I listen to my staff	1	2	3	4
63. I am supportive when staff are upset	1	2	3	4
64. My staff have access to learning about stress management	1	2	3	4
65. I take steps to promote social support amongst the staff group	1	2	3	4
66. I meet regularly with my staff	1	2	3	4
67. Staff in distress have access to professional help	1	2	3	4
68. I am aware of my own feelings and attitudes	1	2	3	4
69. I know my own strengths and needs	1	2	3	4
70. I assert myself	1	2	3	4
71. I elicit feedback on my functioning from my staff	1	2	3	4
72. I link up with other managers	1	2	3	4
73. I set myself clear and reasonable goals	1	2	3	4
74. I reward myself when I have done well	1	2	3	4

75. I enjoy life	1	2	3	4
76. I value myself	1	2	3	4

AREAS OF STRENGTH (items rated 3 or 4)

AREAS OF NEED (items rated 1 or 2)

OUTLINE ACTION PLAN
Priorities for change

Steps to be taken

Time frame/deadlines for actioning steps

APPENDIX 2   Manager's tools—league table

The table is based on the number of chapters in which a tool is mentioned in the Manager's toolkit table at the end of each chapter. It is a frequency count although some of the specific tools mentioned in each chapter have been combined in a single category (for example, *feedback* includes positive, corrective, informational and praise).

This table should be taken in a relatively light hearted fashion:

➤ Frequency of mention is not a direct measure of overall significance
➤ Frequency of mention will reflect the prejudices of the authors as much as the realities of management
➤ The tools themselves are not tightly and exclusively defined or categorised so that scores are to some extent arbitrary (for example *giving feedback* involves *assertiveness* skills, *managing meetings* requires *listening* and *summarising* skills)

However, it does suggest that getting the best out of others involves extensive contact and skilled interaction with those others—that it is definitely a 'hands on' process (not literally of course!). We wonder how that squares with what goes on in many services that are for fellow citizens with long term difficulties and disabilities. As an exercise it might be worth doing time budgeting over a number of weeks and seeing how the league table of time allocations relates to the league table here . . . and thinking about the reasons for any marked discrepancies.

Tool	Frequency of mention
Giving feedback	14
Observation	9
Managing meetings/Problem solving/Decision making	8
Time management/Prioritising	7
Goal setting	6
Modelling	6
Questioning	5
Problem solving	5
Supervision	4
Stating/Giving information/Explaining	4
Mediation/Conflict management	3
Presentation/Teaching	3
Using multimedia communication	3
Task structuring/Analysis	3
Listening	3
Delegating	3
Team building	3
Establishing information/Monitoring systems	3
Job analysis/Descriptions	3
Devise questionnaires	2
Devise individual planning systems	2
Appraisal	2
Persuasion	2
Devise staff competitions	1
Psych up briefings	1
Reflecting	1
Summarising	1
Devising experiments	1
Initiating service review	1
Policy writing	1
Being organised	1
Devise job aids	1
Identify similar services	1
Identify consultants	1
Set group norms	1
Team analysis	1
Reminding	1
Timetabling	1
Having a behavioural vocabulary	1
Recording behaviour	1
Financial management	1
Self management/Control	1
Implementing disciplinary procedures	1
Knowledge about stress	1
Referring on	1
Setting briefs/Contracting	1
Identifying training needs	1
Stress management	1
Assertiveness	1

TEXT REFERENCES
AND FURTHER READING

TEXT REFERENCES

Belbin, R.M. (1981) *Management Teams. Why They Succeed or Fail.* Heinemann.
Dayal, S. and Thomas, J.M. (1968) Operation KPE: developing a new organisation. *Journal of Applied Behavioural Science*, **4**(4), 473–506.

FURTHER READING

Brown, R. (1988) *Group Processes.* Blackwell.
Cooper, C.L., Cooper, R.D. and Eaker, L.H. (1988) *Living with Stress.* Penguin.
Fontana, D. (1990) *Social Skills at Work.* BPS Books. Routledge.
Fontana, D. (1990) *Managing Stress.* BPS Books. Routledge.
Gawlinski, G. and Graessle, L. (1988) *Planning Together. The Art of Effective Teamwork.* Bedford Square Press.
Makin, P., Cooper, C. and Cox, C. (1989) *Managing People at Work.* BPS Books. Routledge.
McLuhan, M. and Fiore, Q. (1967) *The Medium is the Massage.* Penguin.
Peters, T. (1989) *Thriving on Chaos.* Pan Books.
Syer, J. and Connolly, C. (1987) *Sporting Body Sporting Mind.* Sportspages.
Wright, P.L. and Taylor, D.S. (1984) *Improving Leadership Performance.* Prentice Hall International.

INDEX

READER'S NOTEPAD

This book is intended as a source of practical ideas to help mangers to get the best out of their staff. In order to enhance its value as a working resource we have included extra pages so that readers can note down additional information and ideas gathered while using the book.